TOM LACALAMITA

PHOTOGRAPHS BY SIMON METZ

THE
ULTIMATE
BREAD MACHINE
COOKBOOK

SIMON & SCHUSTER

New York   London   Toronto   Sydney   Tokyo   Singapore

SIMON & SCHUSTER
ROCKEFELLER CENTER
1230 AVENUE OF THE AMERICAS
NEW YORK, NY 10020

COPYRIGHT © 1993 BY THOMAS N. LACALAMITA

SIMON & SCHUSTER AND COLOPHON ARE REGISTERED TRADEMARKS
OF SIMON & SCHUSTER INC.

DESIGNED BY EVE METZ
MANUFACTURED IN THE UNITED STATES OF AMERICA

1   3   5   7   9   10   8   6   4   2

LIBRARY OF CONGRESS CATALOGING-IN-PUBLICATION DATA
LACALAMITA, TOM.
THE ULTIMATE BREAD MACHINE COOKBOOK / BY TOM LACALAMITA
P.   CM.
INCLUDES BIBLIOGRAPHICAL REFERENCES AND INDEX.
1. BREAD.   2. AUTOMATIC BREAD MACHINES.   3. COOKERY.
INTERNATIONAL.   I. TITLE
TX769.L24   1993
641.8'15—DC20
ISBN: 0-671-88023-3

PHOTOGRAPHER: SIMON METZ
FOOD STYLIST: A.J. BATTIFARANO
PROP STYLIST: DEBBIE DONAHUE

PROJECT CONSULTANT: KATHERINE SCOTT REISING

FOR YAYI AND CRISTINA

ACKNOWLEDGMENTS

To THE TWO MEN who have taken it upon themselves to make sure that there is a bread machine in every home by the end of the twentieth century. There would be no need for this book if it were not for Aaron Nussbaum and Bernie Sklar and their tireless efforts to spread the word.

To Martha Rodriguez, my recipe tester and special friend, who through good days and the not so good was always there with her measuring cups and spoons and a word of good advice.

To Glenna Vance, a good friend and colleague, for the nutritional analysis and her unending support of bread machines.

To Cecily Brancaccio, for her constant support and enthusiasm.

To Dr. Y. Hironaka, for his interest in this book and his contribution on the history of bread machines in Japan.

To Linda Cunningham, Patty Leasure, and Meaghan Dowling, for transforming a collection of recipes and anecdotes into a book. And to the rest of the Simon & Schuster team, Frank Metz, Mary Bess Engel, Eve Metz, Toni Rachiele, and Joanne Barracca, for their respective contributions along the path of this book's creation.

To Simon Metz and A.J. Battifarano for beautifully portraying these breads on film.

Special thanks to Brian Thornquist of Red Star Yeast and Lee Rafkin of Pillsbury who are the benefactors of the over two thousand loaves of bread that were made for testing the recipes.

And most important, to my family, for sharing with me my love of food; and to my mother, who taught me how to cook.

CONTENTS

PART TWO • HAND-SHAPED DELIGHTS

FOREWORD

FIVE YEARS AGO, food appliance manufacturers and retailers could only wish that bread machines would transform how Americans thought about bread. Today that hopeful vision is a reality, with over two million households owning automatic bread machines and those numbers projected to surpass three million in the near future.

Bread baking is therapeutic, be it by hand or machine. It is an extension of our creativity that produces an edible work of pride. As someone who lives to cook and eat, I am pleased to be considered by some as the "insider" author of automatic bread machine cookbooks. As the product and marketing manager for a leading brand of automatic bread machines, I have been on the cutting edge of the machine's growth and development, participating in its inception and evolution. It is, therefore, with great pleasure that I share some of my favorite recipes and insights with you.

This collection of recipes has been triple-tested in ten basic versions of bread machines and covers all models offered by the leading manufacturers. Having made thousands of loaves of bread, I have developed and fine-tuned these recipes so that they work equally well in all models without the need for adaptations.

When using this cookbook, be sure to measure carefully, use the best ingredients available, and, above all, get to know your bread machine by reading all the materials provided by the manufacturer. I am certain that once you are comfortable with your machine, you will wonder how you ever lived on store-bought bread alone.

INTRODUCTION

WHY AN AUTOMATIC BREAD MACHINE?

I'LL ADMIT I WAS SKEPTICAL the first time I used a bread machine back in 1987. The company I was working for had received a sample of this revolutionary new appliance that was taking Japan by storm and they wanted me to evaluate it over the weekend and give them my comments by Monday morning. I had used a food processor every once in a while to make pizza dough, but an appliance that would do everything from kneading to rising to baking? That was a totally different story. Having baked homemade bread many times, I knew that it was very much a hands-on skill, so how could anyone expect me to believe that an appliance could replace the ritualistic steps with the simple push of a button?

As unconvinced as I was, I was also a little intrigued by the concept, and decided to keep an open mind and experiment with the machine. I decided to go easy on the machine and prepare an ordinary loaf of white bread. The first couple of steps were easy enough. I carefully measured the ingredients, put them in the bread machine, and pushed the "select" button and then "start."

Okay, so it was easy to get the machine started, but I must admit, I remained completely unimpressed. Then, all of a sudden, the ingredients started to blend together into a ball, and the machine was folding the dough over and under again and again, just the way I do it by hand. I still doubted that this sticky white ball of dough could be transformed into a loaf of golden-brown bread with a crispy crust. Needless to say, by the second loaf I was hooked, and over the next few years I would find myself spreading the virtues of automatic bread making nationwide.

Making bread and yeast dough automatically in a bread machine is as much for the uninitiated as it is for the seasoned baker. Depending on the model, you can prepare up to 2 pounds of yeast dough or bread without the trouble and mess that come with handmade breads. And if you have little or no experience working with yeast dough, a bread machine can also be your baking instructor. Since bread machines are preprogrammed, you do not need to know whether or not the dough has been kneaded or has risen long enough. The appliance's microcomputer takes care of those concerns. All you have to worry about is using the ingredients specified in the recipe and measuring accurately. The bread machine does the rest, but you can take all the credit.

Bread Machines: East Meets West

Automatic bread machines were originally developed in Japan for Japanese consumers, not Westerners. Although bread was first introduced in Japan in 1543 by Portuguese explorers and clergy, very few Japanese consumed bread until the nineteenth century, during the end of the Meiji Restoration (1603–1867), when Japan reopened its borders to the outside world after almost three centuries of isolation.

Not all Japanese were impressed with the prospect of having Western influence in their country, and military strife was common during this era. Since bread could be prepared in bakeries, it eventually replaced rice as the food staple on the battlefield. But the influence of bread was short-lived, and it would not be until another military crisis that the Japanese would look to bread as an important form of nourishment.

After World War II, one of the greatest challenges facing the U.S. Occupation Forces in Japan was how to feed the Japanese population during a time of major food shortages. An American-style food service program was developed to feed schoolchildren, who for the first time in their lives ate bread.

In the late 1970s, bread boutiques and bakeries with European-sounding names began popping up all over Japan. Young Japanese were finding breakfast breads and rolls to be more to their liking than a bowl of rice porridge with pickled vegetables. Unfortunately the Japanese only like freshly baked bread, and housewives would have to get up extra early to go out every morning to buy the family's breakfast bread. That was so until electrical engineer Shin Ojima was able to get his invention, a totally automatic bread machine, manufactured. After many false starts, Ojima finally convinced an appliance manufacturer of the merits of his invention, and the first automatic bread machines appeared in Japan in 1987.

Even at prices exceeding $400, automatic bread machines took off, and over one million units were sold in less than twelve months. Then the bottom fell out. You see, most Japanese live in very small apartments and houses with sliding paper-covered walls. And since most people wanted to have their bread ready in the morning, they would use the programmable timer. Well, imagine trying to sleep cuddled up to a bread machine. Between the noise and the aroma, many Japanese families found it difficult sleeping at night and thus abandoned the idea of homemade bread, donating their machines to the rubbish pile.

Fortunately for the Japanese appliance manufacturers, the United States presented a large untapped market, ready and waiting for an appliance like the automatic bread machine.

The first bread machines were sold in the United States in 1988. Originally retailing at $400, they have dropped in price dramatically while the demand has increased steadily, affording millions of Americans the opportunity to make wholesome, nutritious breads with the simple push of a button. The timing of its introduction could not have been better.

BREAD: THE KEY TO A MORE HEALTHFUL DIET

IN 1992, AFTER MANY YEARS of research and planning, the U.S. Government redefined the four basic food groups and introduced the newly designed Food Pyramid. Complex carbohydrates, which consist of grains and cereals, are now the foundation of the pyramid. After years of being told that complex carbohydrates were high in calories, we are now advised that in order to lower the incidence of chronic illnesses like cancer, heart disease, and diabetes, we should increase our consumption of complex carbohydrates by 50 percent and substantially reduce the amount of animal protein, fats, and sugar in our diet. The only problem is, how do we increase our intake of carbohydrates and at the same time maintain an appetizing diet? That's where your bread machine can come in handy.

Since bread derives at least 60 percent of its calories from carbohydrates, it is a healthful, filling food product, usually low in fats and cholesterol, and should be a fundamental part of every diet. By using your automatic bread machine, you can make an endless variety of healthful and nutritious breads for yourself, your family, and your friends.

Healthful bread does not mean heavy whole-grain loaves that can be used as a doorstop. I take great exception to those self-appointed pedagogues who claim that in order for bread to be healthful it can only be made with whole-grain flours. In my opinion, all kinds of breads that are low in fat and cholesterol and that are high in complex carbohydrates should be included in a well-balanced diet consisting of fruits and vegetables and other forms of vegetable protein.

THE INSIDER'S GUIDE TO MAKING BREAD AUTOMATICALLY

WHEN BREAD MACHINES were first introduced, it would have been anyone's guess what kind of popularity they would achieve. Nothing could be more simple than carefully measuring ingredients and pushing a button. However, since the bread machine is an appliance and bread making a chemical reaction among the different ingredients, things can go wrong.

Having made thousands of loaves of bread over the past few years in various machines, I have come to understand how the different bread machines work. I have also picked up many tricks and suggestions as to how to get the machines to perform as expected, and I hope that you will find this information, along with the troubleshooting guide in the last chapter, extremely useful.

First and foremost, take the time to read the owner's manual. It is imperative that you completely understand how your bread machine is programmed to operate. If you have ever made bread by hand, you will understand that recipes often present some variables which bread machine baking cannot fully accommodate. For example, traditional bread recipes often call for varying amounts of flour. A recipe may say, "Add 4 to 6 cups of bread flour depending on the consistency of the dough." Well, 4 to 6 cups is a very wide range. The reason for this inexactitude is that the flour, which can constitute up to 90 percent of the volume of the loaf, contains varying amounts of moisture. Part of this moisture is inherent in the wheat at the time it was harvested and then ground into flour. It can also be affected by ambient humidity, which will raise the moisture content.

When baking by hand, you can touch the dough to determine whether or not it is too sticky and requires additional flour to make it elastic. Since the dough is never touched when making bread automatically in a machine, it is difficult to tell whether or not the dough is the right consistency. If your loaves of bread come out with flat or sunken tops or a coarse crumb, try cutting back on the water by 2 to 4 tablespoons rather than adding additional flour, as you would in traditional bread making. For example, if a recipe calls for ¾ cup, plus 1 tablespoon, try using ¾ cup, less 2 tablespoons. Then let the bread machine knead for 1 to 2 minutes. If the dough appears too dry, go back and add the water you took out, a teaspoon at a time, letting the water knead in after each addition. So that the dough can absorb the water quickly, always add it near the side of the pot. Do not pour the additional water on the dough.

If early in the process you realize that the dough is too sticky, you can add additional flour, a tablespoon at a time, near the side of the pan, while the bread machine is still kneading. Do not add too much flour or the dough will be too heavy and not stretch sufficiently when rising.

If the dough appears dry and crumbly and resembles pie crust or biscuit dough during the first few minutes of the initial kneading cycle, it is too dry and requires additional water. The same is true if the dough divides into two balls during the kneading cycle. To remedy the problem, add additional water, no more than a tablespoon at a time, near the side of the pan, until the dough appears smooth and elastic.

Ambient temperature and that of the ingredients can also affect how the bread machine operates and ultimately how the bread turns out. For best results, all ingredients must be at room temperature, including the water. If your ingredients are too cold, the yeast will not activate properly and the flour will not absorb the liquid ingredients effectively. If the water is too hot, it can kill off the yeast and the bread will not rise as high. Ambient temperature can also affect how the bread comes out. A cold room (lower than 68° F) will make the bread machine cold, which inhibits the dough from rising properly. When the ambient temperature exceeds 80°, the dough may rise inconsistently, with varying outcomes: The dough may rise so high that it touches the lid; it may rise very high and then collapse; or the dough may rise to a normal height, but the crumb will be coarse. When making bread by hand you can easily overcome these problems by popping the bread in the oven once it has doubled in size, but since your bread machine is preprogrammed, you have to let it progress automatically. Therefore the key to consistent results is making sure the ingredients are at room temperature and that the ambient temperature does not exceed 80° or drop lower than 68° F.

Unfortunately, not all bread machines have special programs or indicators that signal when to add ingredients like nuts and dried fruits. If you add them with the primary ingredients at the beginning of the program, they will probably be chopped up, thereby increasing the sugar content of the dough, causing it to rise too much. It is therefore important that these ingredients be added at the appropriate moment. If your bread machine does not have a special program or indicator, add all whole ingredients like nuts, chopped dried fruits, raisins, etc., 8 to 10 minutes before the end of the last kneading cycle. This can be determined easily by looking in the owner's manual.

Bread machine breads look different from what you purchase sliced and packed in plastic bags from the supermarket. In addition, since bread machine bread contains no artificial ingredients and preservatives, it will not stay as "fresh" as preservative-laden store-bought bread. Therefore, make only enough bread for consumption in a 24- to 36-hour period. Homemade breads also have a thicker crust, and this is the way bread should be. Unfortunately, we have been indoctrinated over the years to bread that is mushy and crustless—now is your chance to taste real bread!

For best results in making bread automatically with the push of a button, just remember these few suggestions: Get to know your bread machine by reading the owner's manual. Be willing to experiment until you get the right combination of flour and water. Do not become frustrated if your first attempts do not turn out 100 percent as expected. The odds are that although the bread may not be picture-perfect, it probably tastes great. Also, do not forget that the best source for information on how to use your bread machine is the manufacturer. All bread machine manufacturers have fully staffed customer service departments with trained representatives who are more than happy to answer your questions.

TAKING IT TO THE NEXT STEP

WHILE MUCH EMPHASIS is put on making bread automatically with the push of a button, many people overlook what I believe to be the greatest joy and asset of the bread machine—the "dough/manual" setting for automatically making an endless variety of yeast dough for hand-shaped breads, rolls, sweets, and even lunch and dinner entrées.

As you'll see in Part Two: Hand-Shaped Delights, you can do so much more with a bread machine than just make square or round loaves of bread. And if your baking or cooking skills are limited, don't worry. As long as you played with Play-doh as a child (and I do not know anyone who has not), you will be able to turn out picture-perfect breads and confections in less time than it takes to hop in the car and wait on line at the local bakery on a Sunday morning.

Yeast dough is pretty forgiving. As long as you let it rise sufficiently under the proper conditions, you could not ask for a better sculpting medium to work with. And when you think about it, bread bakers are really artists who use dough.

Most bread machine cookbooks and owner's manuals address the dough or manual cycle as an afterthought. While it makes sense to prepare some loaves of bread automatically before entering the realm of hand-shaping, you should never feel intimidated when working with even the stickiest of doughs, especially since the bread machine will still do all the hard work.

The hand-shaped doughs that you will be working with are somewhat different from those used in the automatic breads section. Some do not have any sugar or fat in them, so the doughs will be more rubbery and require a bit more patience in shaping. Some doughs will have a greater than normal quantity of fats and sweeteners, as with brioche dough. These doughs will require more time to rise before baking (approximately 1 to 2 hours).

Always remember to let the dough rest a few minutes before shaping it. This will allow the gluten, the natural protein found in the wheat, to relax. The dough will then be much more cooperative. If the dough seems to give up again and does not stretch, let it rest another few minutes. Eventually it will give in. Also, always remember to lightly flour your work surface and any utensils you are working with to prevent the dough from sticking.

When making hand-shaped breads, do not become impatient and try to rush the rising process. If the recipe says to let the dough or shaped breads rise until doubled in size, do so. Otherwise the finished product will be smaller than intended and heavy in taste and texture. Always let dough rise in a warm, draft-free location. And always cover the rising dough or bread with a clean kitchen cloth so that it does not dry out.

Once you have mastered these simple recipes, you should be able to take on any yeast dough recipe and adapt it for use in your bread machine. While you should never exceed the manufacturer's maximum amounts for ingredients when making bread automatically, I have found that all bread machines can easily handle up to 3 cups of flour when using the "dough/manual" setting.

INGREDIENTS AND TOOLS OF THE TRADE

ALL BREAD MACHINES appear to perform the same way; however, mechanically, they operate somewhat differently. Some manufacturers require that you first add your active dry yeast, then add the dry ingredients, and then finish up with the liquids. With other manufacturers, it is just the opposite, starting with the liquids and finishing up with the yeast. And one manufacturer offers a special yeast dispenser. In order to facilitate what ingredients to add when, I have divided the ingredients into the following groups: **Yeast, Dry Ingredients, Liquid Ingredients, Fruits, Nuts,** and **Other Ingredients**. Place the ingredient groups into the bread machine in the order specified by the manufacturer in the owner's manual.

Each automatic bread recipe is given for both 2-cup and 3-cup capacity. This refers to the maximum amount of flour recommended by the manufacturer for use in a bread machine. Consult the recipe booklet that came with your bread machine to see how much flour your model uses.

Yeast

Yeast is a tiny, single-cell plant that is used as the leavening agent to make bread rise. Yeast cells are found in the air, and it has been used since the days of the Egyptians. There are basically two types of yeast available to consumers: active dry and fast-rise. Dry yeast is dormant and therefore has a shelf-life of up to 12 months. As long as it is in a factory-sealed package or jar, yeast does not require refrigeration. Once the package is opened, it should either be refrigerated or frozen in an airtight container.

There are thousands of different strains of yeast, and from among these a fast-rising yeast for bread baking was discovered. Yeast uses sugar to create carbon dioxide gas, which gives bread its distinctive small air pockets; however, too much sugar can intoxicate the yeast and slow the rising process. Because fast-rising yeast rises approximately 50 percent more quickly than active dry, its use helps overcome this problem for recipes with a high sugar content, and I have specified its use in some hand-shaped bread recipes. Active dry yeast works best in all other recipes, especially in the automatic bread recipes. Fast-rise yeast can proof too quickly when used in bread machines, with potentially disastrous results, especially during the summer months, when it is hot and humid and the dough will overrise.

Active dry and fast-rise yeasts are available in all supermarkets in 3¼-ounce packet strips or 4-ounce jars. You can also purchase bulk yeast in some warehouse clubs in either 1- or 2-pound packages. I have found that the yeast activity in a recently opened jar or bulk package of yeast is greater than the more commonly available strips. For this reason, you may find it necessary to reduce the amount of yeast specified in the recipe by ¼ to ½ teaspoon the first few times you use jar-packed or bulk yeast.

If you are using bulk yeast that has been opened a few months prior, you may want to check its activity as follows: In a small mixing bowl, dissolve 1 teaspoon of granulated white sugar in ½ cup warm water (110° to 115° F.). Sprinkle 2¼ teaspoons of yeast over the surface. Stir the yeast and let sit for approximately 10 minutes. The yeast mixture should be frothy and doubled in size, which indicates that the yeast activity is still good. If this mixture does not froth and rise, discard and purchase fresh yeast. Since all yeast reacts to temperature and moisture, it is important that all the ingredients in the recipe be at room temperature and the ambient temperature be no lower than 65° F. and no higher than 80° F.

Flour

Wheat is the only grain that has a high enough protein content (gluten) to make it ideal for making bread. As dough is kneaded and the gluten comes in contact with the recipe's liquid ingredients, an interlocking network of elastic strands is formed, which traps the carbon dioxide created by the yeast. As you continue to knead the dough, the gluten network increases and strengthens the dough, allowing it to support the height and width of the loaf. Different types of wheat when milled produce different types of flour with varying gluten levels. Flours milled from hard or winter wheat have the highest gluten content, and they are marketed in the supermarket in 5-pound sacks labeled "bread flour." I strongly recommend using these flours when making breads in a bread machine, since in all of my testing, flours high in gluten performed the best.

If you are unable to locate bread flour in your local supermarket, it can be ordered by telephone or mail from the companies listed at the end of the book. Unbleached all-purpose flour from the supermarket can also be used, but this flour's lower gluten content will not produce the high, well-rounded loaves of bread that you get with bread flour. You can, however, try some of the unbleached, all-purpose flours milled in small batches and available by mail. My results with these flours were as good as with high-gluten bread flour.

Whole-wheat flour is milled from 100 percent of the wheat kernel. Many find that bread made from the whole-wheat flour available in supermarkets is bitter-tasting and coarse, which does not make for an exceptional loaf of bread. Furthermore, whole-wheat flour requires more kneading to absorb liquid, and since most bread machines are preprogrammed, 100 percent whole-wheat bread does not turn out well on the automatic bread program. For these reasons, I strongly recommend one of two things: either mix supermarket-purchased whole-wheat flour with white bread flour, or order by mail 100 percent white whole-wheat flour from Kansas or 100 percent golden wheat, both of which are made from new strains of wheat that are milled from 100 percent of the kernel and are lighter in color, taste, and texture.

Keep in mind that since wheat is organic, the quality of the crop can vary from harvest to harvest. While the flour mills blend different types of wheat to maintain certain standards and levels of protein (gluten) and moisture, variations that can affect how your bread comes out can and do occur. In preparing the recipes for this book, I have tried to take into account some of these variables. Nevertheless, if you find that all of a sudden you begin to see radically different baking results, do not become alarmed. It may very well be that the flour you are using has a lower-than-normal protein level and a higher level of moisture. Try switching brands of flour or add an additional teaspoon of lemon juice to the recipe. You may also wish to try a dough enhancer; these are available through some mail order catalogues (see page 201). Dough enhancers usually contain all-natural ingredients, such as dried whey, malt powder, and vegetable gluten, and help to fortify the dough to rise better.

All other flours, including rye and buckwheat, are either very low in gluten or have none whatsoever. They therefore must be blended with wheat flour in order to make bread.

To measure flour accurately, never dip the measuring cup into the bag of flour, since air pockets can occur and you may not get a full cup of flour. Spoon the flour, a tablespoon at a time, into the measuring cup. Stick a blunt-ended knife into the flour a couple of times to break up any air pockets or clumps. Level off with the knife.

Liquids

The liquid ingredients bind the dry ingredients together. While water is usually the most common liquid used in making bread, recipes can also call for milk, eggs, and fruit juices. Even though puréed fruits and vegetables are not really liquids, they are included in the liquid section of the recipes, since they add moisture to the dough.

All water is not treated equally, and I mean that literally. Since drinking water is chemically treated, certain chemicals can adversely affect the yeast. Water that is high in fluoride and chlorine can slow down the rising process, resulting in low, stubby loaves. If your breads are not rising well, either boil and cool your water before using it or try bottled spring water. Hard water will also slow down the rising process, and soft water can cause "sticky-dough syndrome." Try a different source of water for better results.

Most of the recipes in this book call for nonfat dry milk rather than liquid milk. The simple reason is that bread machines bake at an intense heat level and liquid milk can scorch and darken the color of the bread crust. Nonfat dry milk is available in every supermarket in the same aisle as canned milk. Milk gives bread a softer, ivory-colored crumb. Buttermilk makes bread moister, as do potatoes and potato water.

Eggs add color and protein, and strengthen the dough. Always use large eggs whenever called for in the recipe. A large egg adds approximately ¼ cup of liquid. Medium eggs can cause the dough to be too dry. Extra-large and jumbo eggs will add too much moisture and the dough will be too wet.

Lemon juice is an interesting additive to bread. Since gluten can vary from sack to sack, lemon juice helps to strengthen and enhance the dough, providing greater consistency, especially when making automatic breads, without changing the flavor.

Sweeteners

Although sweeteners (granulated white sugar, brown sugar, honey, and molasses) are not needed to make bread, they can give breads additional flavor and color. Since sweeteners can caramelize during baking, you do not want to add too much, especially if you are baking the bread in the bread machine. If your bread is coming out too dark or burning, decrease the amount of sweetener and, if possible, set the bread machine on a lighter setting. You can also substitute sugar with liquid sweeteners like honey and molasses. Just be sure to reduce the amount of liquid called for in the recipe by the same amount of liquid sweetener in order to keep the absorption ratio of dry and liquid ingredients the same.

Salt

Although you can get away without using salt when making bread by hand, I find that just a little salt is essential when making bread automatically in a bread machine since it slightly inhibits the rising action of the yeast, and therefore keeps the dough under control.

Fats

Butter, margarine, shortening, or oil add richness to the flavor of bread and help to keep bread fresher longer. Nevertheless, there are also many breads that contain no additional fats at all.

Fruit, Nuts, and Other Ingredients

You can easily change the taste and look of a basic bread recipe by adding ingredients like chopped dried fruits, nuts, shredded cheeses, spices, and herbs. Always add ingredients like dried fruits and nuts at the moment appropriate for your model of bread machine. Cheese, herbs, and spices can be added at the beginning when you add your dry ingredients. When using cheese in automatic bread recipes, be sure that it is mild. I have found that sharp cheese can cause the dough to rise too quickly and then collapse. This is most probably due to the enzymes that certain sharp cheeses contain. Specialty ingredients like flavored oils, herbs, and spices can be ordered by mail from specialty catalogues.

Tools of the Trade

Since you have already invested in a bread machine, you might as well go the extra mile and spend a few dollars more to equip yourself with the necessary baking accessories to make your life a lot easier and your breads even more professional looking. Most of these accessories are available in any good housewares store.

Measuring Cups and Spoons

Please do not use coffee cups and eating utensils to measure ingredients. These are not standard measures. If you do not own U.S. standard measuring cups, purchase easy-to-read plastic or metal ones in ¼-, ⅓-, ½-, ⅔-, ¾-, and 1-cup capacities. Also measuring spoons in ¼-, ½-, and 1-teaspoon capacities and ½ and 1 tablespoon.

Instant Read Thermometer

Many bread recipes tell you that the bread is ready when you tap the bottom of a baked loaf and you hear a dull thud. This is as accurate as telling fortunes. When an instant read thermometer is inserted into a loaf of hand-shaped bread straight from the oven, it gives you the internal temperature reading. A baked loaf of bread should be between 190° to 195° F. This is a surefire way to know that your hand-shaped loaves are baked to perfection.

Baking Pans

I personally prefer good old heavy-gauge aluminum baking pans. The nonstick and dark-colored ones tend to cause the breads to brown too quickly.

Parchment Paper

This wonderful moisture- and grease-resistant paper, available in rolls in most housewares stores, makes clean-up a breeze. Cut a piece large enough to cover your baking pan. Place dough directly on parchment paper without greasing the pan, thus eliminating the need to wash the pan after use.

Baking Stone and Tiles

Since most of us cannot afford the luxury of having a steam-injected, clay and brick oven installed in our kitchens, we can enjoy the next best thing to making wonderful hand-shaped loaves of crisp crust, chewy bread. Clay or composition baking stones or tiles can be placed either on the bottom of a cold oven or on the lowest rack setting. As the oven heats up, so do the tiles. The bread is then baked directly on them. Since they are unglazed and porous, the tiles will draw moisture from the bread as it is baking. The result is beyond words, especially if you happen to spray the sides of the hot oven a few times with clean, cool water while the bread is baking.

Baker's Peel

If you plan to use a baking stone or tiles you will also need a baker's peel. This flat paddle is made of wood. After sprinkling with either flour or cornmeal, place shaped loaves of bread on the peel or use as a work surface to prepare pizzas. The peel assists in sliding breads and pizzas into the oven directly onto the preheated baking stones or tiles. It should also be used for removing them.

Spray Bottle

As mentioned above, spraying the sides of a hot oven while the bread is baking helps to give it a crisp crust. Pick up an inexpensive, pump-type spray bottle in any dime store.

PART ONE

BREAD AUTOMATICALLY WITH THE PUSH OF A BUTTON

BASIC BREADS

HEARTY GRAIN AND HIGH-FIBER BREADS

OLD-FASHIONED COUNTRY AND CELEBRATION BREADS

Basic Breads

Basic breads are the easiest to make in your automatic bread machine. Made primarily with white bread flour, these breads rise almost to the top of the bread pan and bake into a chewy loaf with a nice thin crust.

Many people incorrectly believe that breads made with white flour have little or no nutritive value. White wheat flour (all-purpose bleached and unbleached, and bread flour) is milled from the endosperm of the wheat kernel; it has a creamy white color because this endosperm is separated from the bran and germ. The endosperm makes up 83 percent of the wheat kernel and contains the greatest percentage of protein, carbohydrates, and iron as well as many B-complex vitamins, such as riboflavin, niacin, and thiamine, all of which are essential for good health. And although breads made from white flour are lower in dietary fiber than 100 percent whole-wheat bread, 4 ounces of white bread (approximately four slices) contain more dietary fiber than an equivalent serving of lettuce or apples.

While a good source of complex carbohydrates, breads made from white flour also provide a valuable source of soluble fibers which help lower cholesterol.

By adding other ingredients such as other types of grains, dried fruits, vegetables, and dairy products, the nutritive value, not to mention the taste, of breads made with white flour becomes even more healthful and better for you. So remember, there is no reason to ever apologize again for enjoying a good slice of homemade bread made with white flour.

WHITE BREAD

The bread of choice for generations of Americans, white bread has recently become much maligned and criticized for its supposed lack of nutritional value compared with full fiber breads. Unfortunately, many commercial bread producers have given us a hybrid version of white bread that is tasteless and without substance. The recipe given here is for white bread as it should be. Chewy with a thin, crisp crust, this bread is high in complex carbohydrates and has less than 1 gram of fat per slice.

2-CUP CAPACITY 12 SERVINGS	INGREDIENTS	3-CUP CAPACITY 16 SERVINGS
	YEAST	
1½ teaspoons	Active dry yeast	2¼ teaspoons
	DRY INGREDIENTS	
2 cups	Bread flour	3 cups
¾ teaspoon	Salt	1 teaspoon
2 teaspoons	Granulated white sugar	1 tablespoon
2 tablespoons plus 1 teaspoon	Nonfat dry milk	4 tablespoons
2 teaspoons	Unsalted butter or margarine	1 tablespoon
	LIQUID INGREDIENTS	
¾ cup plus 1 tablespoon	Water	1¼ cups
1 teaspoon	Lemon juice	1 teaspoon

All ingredients must be at room temperature, unless otherwise noted. Add ingredients in the order specified in your bread machine owner's manual. Set bread machine on the basic/standard bread making setting. Select medium or normal baking cycle. The programmable timer can be used, if desired.

Nutrition information per ½-inch slice:
88 calories, 2.56 g protein, 17.0 g carbohydrates, 0.66 g dietary fiber, 0.86 g fat, 1.87 mg cholesterol, 139 mg sodium, 43.0 mg potassium. Calories from protein: 12%; from carbohydrates: 79%; from fats: 9%.

WHITE BREAD VARIATIONS

By ADDING other ingredients, herbs, and spices, basic white bread can take on an endless variety of guises. The following are a few suggestions.

VEGETABLE BREAD

Dehydrated vegetables such as carrots, celery, onions, tomatoes, and peppers make a great addition to homemade bread, and can be found in the spice section of most supermarkets. Vegetable bread sliced thin and spread with cream cheese makes an interesting sandwich or appetizer.

2-Cup Capacity: Add ¼ cup mixed dehydrated vegetables to the basic 2-Cup White Bread recipe. Increase water by 1 tablespoon. Do not use the programmable timer, since the vegetables will absorb the water. 12 SERVINGS

3-Cup Capacity: Add ⅓ cup mixed dehydrated vegetables to the basic 3-Cup White Bread recipe. Increase water by 1½ tablespoons. Do not use the programmable timer, since the vegetables will absorb the water. 16 SERVINGS

> **Nutrition information per ½-inch slice:**
> 103 calories, 3.04 g protein, 19.9 g carbohydrates, 0.95 g dietary fiber, 0.95 g fat, 2.13 mg cholesterol, 143 mg sodium, 75.3 mg potassium. Calories from protein: 12%; from carbohydrates: 79%; from fats: 9%.

BACON CORN BREAD

Crisp-fried slab bacon, coarsely ground cornmeal, and frozen corn kernels add a real country flavor to basic white bread.

2-Cup Capacity: Add 2 tablespoons coarsely ground cornmeal and 2 tablespoons crisp-fried slab bacon cut into ¼-inch chunks to the basic 2-Cup White Bread recipe. Increase water by 1½ teaspoons. Add ¼ cup frozen corn kernels and 1 tablespoon bread flour at the appropriate moment for your model bread machine. 12 SERVINGS

3-Cup Capacity: Add 3 tablespoons coarsely ground cornmeal and 3 tablespoons crisp-fried slab bacon cut into ¼-inch chunks to the basic 3-Cup White Bread recipe. Increase water by 2 teaspoons. Add ⅓ cup frozen corn kernels and 1½ tablespoons bread flour at the appropriate moment for your model bread machine. 16 SERVINGS

> **Nutrition information per ½-inch slice:**
> 112 calories, 3.44 g protein, 20.5 g carbohydrates, 0.88 g dietary fiber, 1.57 g fat, 3.13 mg cholesterol, 159 mg sodium, 59.8 mg potassium. Calories from protein: 13%; from carbohydrates: 75%; from fats: 13%.

WHEAT BREAD

Milled from the whole kernel, whole-wheat flour contains all of the bran and fiber of the kernel making it extremely high in insoluble fiber, which is essential for a well-balanced diet.

Red wheat flour is the most widely available whole-wheat flour; however, its texture is coarse and its flavor bitter. One option is to mix this flour with refined white flour, thereby taming the texture and flavor, although this is not 100 percent whole wheat.

Some alternatives available through specialty catalogues are white whole-wheat flour, which comes from Kansas, and golden wheat flour, which is from Montana. Lighter in flavor and color, these contain as much fiber as red wheat but produce far superior loaves of whole-grain bread.

Since you may wish to use the whole-wheat flour available in your local supermarket, I have formulated the following recipe using the mixture of bread flour and whole wheat. If you decide to use one of the lighter whole-wheat flours, you can substitute this for the bread flour.

2-CUP CAPACITY 12 SERVINGS	INGREDIENTS	3-CUP CAPACITY 16 SERVINGS
	YEAST	
1½ teaspoons	Active dry yeast	2¼ teaspoons
	DRY INGREDIENTS	
1½ cups	Bread flour	2¼ cups
½ cup	Whole-wheat flour	¾ cup
1 teaspoon	Salt	1½ teaspoons
2 tablespoons, plus 2 teaspoons	Nonfat dry milk	4 tablespoons
2 teaspoons	Unsalted butter or margarine	1 tablespoon
	LIQUID INGREDIENTS	
½ cup, plus 1 tablespoon	Water	1 cup
2 tablespoons	Honey	3 tablespoons
1 large	Egg	1 large
1 teaspoon	Lemon juice	1 teaspoon

All ingredients must be at room temperature, unless otherwise noted. Add ingredients in the order specified in your bread machine owner's manual. Set bread machine on the basic/standard bread making setting. Select medium or normal baking cycle except for Panasonic/National models, which should be set on light. Do not use the programmable timer when making this bread since the recipe contains perishable ingredients.

HINT: If dough appears too dry after kneading for the first couple of minutes, add water, no more than 1 tablespoon at a time, just until dough appears elastic. Do not add too much water.

Nutrition information per ½-inch slice:
111 calories, 3.51 g protein, 21.4 g carbohydrates, 1.31 g dietary fiber, 1.32 g fat, 15.4 mg cholesterol, 211 mg sodium, 74.1 mg potassium. Calories from protein: 13%; from carbohydrates: 76%; from fats: 11%.

RYE BREAD

Where would corned beef and pastrami be without rye bread? Rye flour, which is milled from the rye plant, is very low in gluten and therefore must be mixed with bread flour for best results. Well-made rye bread has a chewy crumb and crust. The addition of coarsely ground cornmeal and caraway seeds adds extra flavor and crunch.

2-CUP CAPACITY 12 SERVINGS	INGREDIENTS	3-CUP CAPACITY 16 SERVINGS
	YEAST	
1½ teaspoons	Active dry yeast	2¼ teaspoons
	DRY INGREDIENTS	
1⅓ cups	Bread flour	2 cups
⅔ cup	Medium rye flour	1 cup
1 tablespoon	Coarsely ground cornmeal	1½ tablespoons
½ teaspoon	Caraway seeds	1 teaspoon
1 teaspoon	Salt	1½ teaspoons
2 teaspoons	Dark brown sugar	1 tablespoon
4 teaspoons	Unsalted butter or margarine	2 tablespoons
OPTIONAL:		
1 tablespoon	Dehydrated onion flakes	1½ tablespoons
	LIQUID INGREDIENTS	
½ cup	Water	¾ cup
¼ cup, plus 2 tablespoons	Buttermilk	½ cup

All ingredients must be at room temperature, unless otherwise noted. Add ingredients in the order specified in your bread machine owner's manual. Set bread machine on the basic/standard bread making setting. Select medium or normal baking cycle. Do not use the programmable timer when making this bread since the recipe contains perishable ingredients.

Nutrition information per ½-inch slice:
92.9 calories, 2.44 g protein, 16.9 g carbohydrates, 1.39 g dietary fiber, 1.61 g fat, 3.73 mg cholesterol, 187 mg sodium, 62.0 mg potassium. Calories from protein: 10%; from carbohydrates: 74%; from fats: 16%.

White Bread (page 28)

Wheat Bread (page 30)

Rye Bread (page 32)

Onion Egg Bread (page 38)

Olive Oil Garlic Bread (page 40)

Carolina Rice Bread (page 43)

Pesto Bread (page 44)

EGG BREAD

Egg bread is very practical. Dipped in beaten egg, sautéed, and served with maple syrup it can become French toast. At lunchtime it can be spread with mustard and layered with your favorite cold cuts or cheese. For a light supper, slice thin, toast, and cover with smoked salmon, chopped onions, and capers. And if by some remote possibility you have any leftover egg bread that goes stale, dice it up to use as poultry stuffing.

2-CUP CAPACITY 12 SERVINGS	INGREDIENTS	3-CUP CAPACITY 16 SERVINGS
	YEAST	
1½ teaspoons	Active dry yeast	2¼ teaspoons
	DRY INGREDIENTS	
2 cups	Bread flour	3 cups
¾ teaspoon	Salt	1 teaspoon
2 teaspoons	Dark brown sugar	1 tablespoon
2 tablespoons, plus 1 teaspoon	Nonfat dry milk	4 tablespoons
4 teaspoons	Unsalted butter or margarine	2 tablespoons
	LIQUID INGREDIENTS	
½ cup, less 1 teaspoon	Water	1 cup, less 1½ tablespoons
1 teaspoon	Vanilla extract	1½ teaspoons
1 large	Egg	1 large
0	Egg yolk	1
1 teaspoon	Lemon juice	1 teaspoon

All ingredients must be at room temperature, unless otherwise noted. Add ingredients in the order specified in your bread machine owner's manual. Set bread machine on the basic/standard bread making setting. If possible, select light baking cycle. If not, use medium or normal baking cycle. Do not use the programmable timer when making this bread since the recipe contains perishable ingredients.

> **Nutrition information per ½-inch slice:**
> 100 calories, 3.09 g protein, 17.1 g carbohydrates, 0.66 g dietary fiber, 1.91 g fat, 21.3 mg cholesterol, 144 mg sodium, 50.8 mg potassium. Calories from protein: 12%; from carbohydrates: 70%; from fats: 18%

Seven-Grain Millet Bread (page 46)

BUTTERMILK BREAD

Buttermilk bread reminds me of sourdough white bread without the trouble of having to prepare and replenish the starter. Buttermilk gives the loaf a nice ivory crumb, chewy texture, and slight tartness. It is a great all-purpose bread for sandwiches or toast.

2-CUP CAPACITY 12 SERVINGS	INGREDIENTS	3-CUP CAPACITY 16 SERVINGS
	YEAST	
1½ teaspoons	Active dry yeast	2¼ teaspoons
	DRY INGREDIENTS	
2 cups	Bread flour	3 cups
¾ teaspoon	Salt	1 teaspoon
4 teaspoons	Dark brown sugar	2 tablespoons
4 teaspoons	Unsalted butter or margarine	2 tablespoons
	LIQUID INGREDIENTS	
¼ cup, plus 3 tablespoons	Water	¾ cup
¼ cup, plus 2 tablespoons	Buttermilk	½ cup
1 teaspoon	Lemon juice	1 teaspoon

All ingredients must be at room temperature, unless otherwise noted. Add ingredients in the order specified in your bread machine owner's manual. Set bread machine on the basic/standard bread making setting. Select medium or normal baking cycle. Do not use the programmable timer when making this bread since the recipe contains perishable ingredients.

Nutrition information per ½-inch slice:
96.7 calories, 2.53 g protein, 17.7 g carbohydrates, 0.66 g dietary fiber, 1.5 g fat, 3.73 mg cholesterol, 143 mg sodium, 45.9 mg potassium. Calories from protein: 10%; from carbohydrates: 75%; from fats: 15%.

CINNAMON RAISIN BREAD

Nothing compares to the comforting aroma of a loaf of cinnamon raisin bread baking. It brightens up even the gloomiest of days.

Be sure to add the raisins at the specified moment or they will be chopped up into tiny particles during the kneading process.

2-CUP CAPACITY 12 SERVINGS	INGREDIENTS	3-CUP CAPACITY 16 SERVINGS
	YEAST	
1½ teaspoons	Active dry yeast	2¼ teaspoons
	DRY INGREDIENTS	
2 cups	Bread flour	3 cups
¾ teaspoon	Ground cinnamon	1 teaspoon
¾ teaspoon	Salt	1 teaspoon
2 teaspoons	Dark brown sugar	1 tablespoon
2 tablespoons, plus 1 teaspoon	Nonfat dry milk	4 tablespoons
2 teaspoons	Unsalted butter or margarine	1 tablespoon
	LIQUID INGREDIENTS	
¾ cup, plus 1 tablespoon	Water	1¼ cups
1 teaspoon	Lemon juice	1 teaspoon
	RAISINS	
⅓ cup	Raisins	½ cup

All ingredients must be at room temperature, unless otherwise noted. Add ingredients in the order specified in your bread machine owner's manual. Add **raisins** at the appropriate moment for your model bread machine. Set bread machine on the basic/standard bread making setting. Select medium or normal baking cycle. The programmable timer can be used, if desired.

Nutrition information per ½-inch slice:
100 calories, 2.69 g protein, 20.4 g carbohydrates, 0.93 g dietary fiber, 0.88 g fat, 1.87 mg cholesterol, 140 mg sodium, 76.3 mg potassium. Calories from protein: 11%; from carbohydrates: 81%; from fats: 8%.

POTATO BREAD

Potato bread was very popular on the prairie. At times potatoes were used to stretch a meager amount of flour to produce larger quantities of bread. They also gave it a rich, soft texture and a thin, crisp crust.

For variation, try adding either caraway seeds or snipped fresh chives.

Allow at least one hour before making this bread to prepare the mashed potatoes.

2-CUP CAPACITY 12 SERVINGS	INGREDIENTS	3-CUP CAPACITY 16 SERVINGS
	YEAST	
1½ teaspoons	Active dry yeast	2¼ teaspoons
	DRY INGREDIENTS	
2 cups	Bread flour	3 cups
1 teaspoon	Salt	1½ teaspoons
2 teaspoons	Granulated white sugar	1 tablespoon
2 tablespoons	Nonfat dry milk	3 tablespoons
4 teaspoons	Unsalted butter or margarine	2 tablespoons
OPTIONAL:		
½ teaspoon	Caraway seeds	¾ teaspoon
OR:		
2 teaspoons	Snipped, fresh chives	3 teaspoons
	LIQUID INGREDIENTS	
½ cup	Plain, mashed potatoes (see note)	¾ cup
½ cup, plus 2 teaspoons	Reserved potato water	¾ cup, plus 1 tablespoon
1 teaspoon	Lemon juice	1 teaspoon

All ingredients must be at room temperature, unless otherwise noted. Add ingredients in the order specified in your bread machine owner's manual. Set bread machine on the basic/standard bread making setting. Select medium or normal baking cycle. Do not use the programmable timer when making this bread since the recipe contains ingredients that can absorb the water prior to the start of the bread making process.

NOTE: To make mashed potatoes for 2-cup-capacity recipe, peel and quarter a medium 4-ounce red potato. Boil until tender in unsalted water. Drain, reserving water. Mash potato with a fork until smooth. Cool to room temperature before using. For 3-cup-capacity recipe, peel and quarter a large 6-ounce red potato. Follow same procedure.

HINT: If dough appears too dry after kneading for the first couple of minutes, add potato water, no more than 1 tablespoon at a time, just until dough appears elastic. Do not add too much water.

Nutrition information per ½-inch slice:
100 calories, 2.71 g protein, 18.6 g carbohydrates, 0.81 g dietary fiber, 1.56 g fat, 3.74 mg cholesterol, 209 mg sodium, 69.0 mg potassium. Calories from protein: 11%; from carbohydrates: 75%; from fats: 14%.

ONION EGG BREAD

Sunday morning is a special time at our house since it is the only morning of the week that we can have a leisurely breakfast as a family. We usually prepare breakfast together, or visit our favorite local bakery and get some of those great onion egg rolls that Cristina, my daughter, likes so much. This recipe was inspired by those rolls. Rich in flavor and aroma, this bread is great as is or, better yet, with some of last night's leftover roast chicken and a little mayo.

2-CUP CAPACITY 12 SERVINGS	INGREDIENTS	3-CUP CAPACITY 16 SERVINGS
	YEAST	
1½ teaspoons	Active dry yeast	2¼ teaspoons
	DRY INGREDIENTS	
2 cups	Bread flour	3 cups
2 tablespoons	Dehydrated onion flakes	3 tablespoons
1 teaspoon	Poppy seeds	1½ teaspoons
¾ teaspoon	Salt	1 teaspoon
2 teaspoons	Granulated white sugar	1 tablespoon
2 tablespoons, plus 1 teaspoon	Nonfat dry milk	4 tablespoons
4 teaspoons	Unsalted butter or margarine	2 tablespoons
	LIQUID INGREDIENTS	
½ cup, plus 1 tablespoon	Water	1 cup
1 large	Egg	1 large
1 teaspoon	Lemon juice	1 teaspoon

All ingredients must be at room temperature, unless otherwise noted. Add ingredients in the order specified in your bread machine owner's manual. Set bread machine on the basic/standard bread making setting. Select medium or normal baking cycle. Do not use the programmable timer when making this bread since the recipe contains perishable ingredients.

Nutrition information per ½-inch slice:
103 calories, 3.18 g protein, 17.6 g carbohydrates, 0.73 g dietary fiber, 2.02 g fat, 21.3 mg cholesterol, 144 mg sodium, 59.4 mg potassium. Calories from protein: 12%; from carbohydrates: 70%; from fats: 18%.

BUCKWHEAT MOLASSES BREAD

This is one of my favorite breads, with the buckwheat adding a gentle flavor of goodness and the molasses a mellow smoothness.

Interestingly enough, buckwheat is not even a grain. Originally a wild meadow plant, this low green plant with white flowers produces tiny seeds that are milled into buckwheat flour. It is highly prized by the Japanese who use it to make soba noodles, and by the Russians who use it to make blinis.

2-CUP CAPACITY 12 SERVINGS	INGREDIENTS	3-CUP CAPACITY 16 SERVINGS
	YEAST	
1½ teaspoons	Active dry yeast	2¼ teaspoons
	DRY INGREDIENTS	
2 cups	Bread flour	3 cups
½ cup	Light buckwheat flour	¾ cup
¾ teaspoon	Salt	1 teaspoon
2 tablespoons, plus 1 teaspoon	Nonfat dry milk	4 tablespoons
2 teaspoons	Unsalted butter or margarine	1 tablespoon
	LIQUID INGREDIENTS	
½ cup	Water	¾ cup, plus 2 tablespoons
1 large	Egg	1 large
4 teaspoons	Molasses	2 tablespoons

All ingredients must be at room temperature, unless otherwise noted. Add ingredients in the order specified in your bread machine owner's manual. Set bread machine on the basic/standard bread making setting. Select medium or normal baking cycle. Do not use the programmable timer when making this bread since the recipe contains perishable ingredients.

Nutrition information per ½-inch slice:
97.1 calories, 2.69 g protein, 19.2 g carbohydrates, 0.79 g dietary fiber, 0.88 g fat, 1.87 mg cholesterol, 139 mg sodium, 69.9 mg potassium. Calories from protein: 11%; from carbohydrates: 80%; from fats: 8%.

OLIVE OIL GARLIC BREAD

In ancient Greek mythology Zeus uses the olive branch as a symbol of life. This association could not be more appropriate, since olive oil is a natural product of the earth with many nutritive properties.

This fragrant bread, made from garlic-infused olive oil, is delicious when lightly toasted, covered with sun-ripened tomatoes and basil and drizzled with extra-virgin olive oil.

My recipe for garlic olive oil follows but, if you don't have the time, it is available at certain supermarkets or specialty food stores. If making the garlic olive oil at home, do so the day before you plan to make this bread, since the garlic should steep in the oil for at least 6 hours before using.

2-CUP CAPACITY 12 SERVINGS	INGREDIENTS	3-CUP CAPACITY 16 SERVINGS
	YEAST	
1½ teaspoons	Active dry yeast	2¼ teaspoons
	DRY INGREDIENTS	
2 cups	Bread flour	3 cups
1 teaspoon	Salt	1½ teaspoons
2 teaspoons	Granulated white sugar	1 tablespoon
	LIQUID INGREDIENTS	
½ cup, plus 2 tablespoons	Water	1 cup
3 tablespoons	Garlic olive oil (see note)	¼ cup

All ingredients must be at room temperature, unless otherwise noted. Add ingredients in the order specified in your bread machine owner's manual. Set bread machine on the basic/standard bread making setting. Select medium or normal baking cycle. The programmable timer can be used, if desired.

NOTE:
Garlic Olive Oil
⅓ cup peeled garlic cloves, slightly crushed
1 cup extra-virgin olive oil

To make the garlic olive oil, heat the extra-virgin olive oil in a small, heavy-bottomed saucepan over medium heat. When the oil begins to smoke, remove from heat immediately and let cool for 10 minutes. Add the prepared garlic cloves. Let steep for at least six hours at room temperature. Remove garlic cloves from oil and discard. Store any unused garlic oil in the refrigerator for up to seven days.

Nutrition information per ½-inch slice:
109 calories, 2.26 g protein, 16.6 g carbohydrates, 0.66 g dietary fiber, 3.58 g fat, 0 mg cholesterol, 179 mg sodium, 28.7 mg potassium. Calories from protein: 8%; from carbohydrates: 62%; from fats: 30%.

SHAKER HERB BREAD

One of the few pleasures allowed by the Shakers, besides singing and dancing, was eating. Shaker sisters were experts in the kitchen, especially when it came to herbs, which were used in numerous combinations, as in this fragrant Shaker herb bread.

2-CUP CAPACITY 12 SERVINGS	INGREDIENTS	3-CUP CAPACITY 16 SERVINGS
	YEAST	
1½ teaspoons	Active dry yeast	2¼ teaspoons
	DRY INGREDIENTS	
2 cups	Bread flour	3 cups
½ teaspoon	Celery seed	¾ teaspoon
½ teaspoon	Caraway seed	¾ teaspoon
½ teaspoon	Ground sage	¾ teaspoon
½ teaspoon	Ground nutmeg	¾ teaspoon
1 teaspoon	Salt	1½ teaspoons
2 teaspoons	Granulated white sugar	1 tablespoon
2 tablespoons	Nonfat dry milk	4 tablespoons
2 teaspoons	Unsalted butter or margarine	1 tablespoon
	LIQUID INGREDIENTS	
½ cup, plus 1 tablespoon	Water	1 cup
1 large	Egg	1 large
1 teaspoon	Lemon juice	1 teaspoon

All ingredients must be at room temperature, unless otherwise noted. Add ingredients in the order specified in your bread machine owner's manual. Set bread machine on the basic/standard bread making setting. Select medium or normal baking cycle. Do not use the programmable timer when making this bread since the recipe contains perishable ingredients.

Nutrition information per ½-inch slice:
106 calories, 3.38 g protein, 19.4 g carbohydrates, 0.8 g dietary fiber, 1.36 g fat, 15.4 mg cholesterol, 211 mg sodium, 58.7 mg potassium. Calories from protein: 13%; from carbohydrates: 75%; from fats: 12%.

CAROLINA RICE BREAD

The rice, which blends into the dough, adds flavor and texture, giving this great all-purpose bread a crisp, golden-brown crust and ivory white crumb. Allow extra time when making this bread to prepare the rice.

2-CUP CAPACITY 12 SERVINGS	INGREDIENTS	3-CUP CAPACITY 16 SERVINGS
	YEAST	
1½ teaspoons	Active dry yeast	2¼ teaspoons
	DRY INGREDIENTS	
2 cups	Bread flour	3 cups
1 teaspoon	Salt	1½ teaspoons
2 teaspoons	Granulated white sugar	1 tablespoon
4 teaspoons	Nonfat dry milk	2 tablespoons
1½ teaspoons	Unsalted butter or margarine	1 tablespoon
	LIQUID INGREDIENTS	
½ cup	Well-cooked, white rice (see note)	¾ cup
½ cup	Water	¾ cup
1 large	Egg	1 large
1 teaspoon	Lemon juice	1 teaspoon

All ingredients must be at room temperature, unless otherwise noted. Add ingredients in the order specified in your bread machine owner's manual. Set bread machine on the basic/standard bread making setting. Select medium or normal baking cycle. Do not use the programmable timer when making this bread since the recipe contains perishable ingredients.

NOTE: To make rice: For 2-cup-capacity recipe, bring ¾ cup of unsalted water to a boil. Add ¼ cup raw long-grain white rice. Cover and let simmer until very soft and kernel ends begin to split. Drain well. Cool to room temperature before using. For 3-cup-capacity recipe, use 1 cup unsalted water and ¼ cup plus 2 tablespoons raw long-grain white rice. Follow same procedure.

Nutrition information per ½-inch slice:
103 calories, 3.18 g protein, 19.3 g carbohydrates, 0.69 g dietary fiber, 1.13 g fat, 19.1 mg cholesterol, 186 mg sodium, 45.2 mg potassium. Calories from protein: 13%; from carbohydrates: 77%; from fats: 10%.

PESTO BREAD

Pesto is a fresh herb sauce that is made from basil leaves, garlic, pine nuts, grated Pecorino Romano cheese, and extra-virgin olive oil.

While this sauce is usually served with pasta or minestrone, it can also transform a loaf of bread into a fragrant bouquet. With a light crumb and crisp crust, pesto bread is a natural companion to any Italian meal.

Prepared pesto sauce is popping up more and more in supermarket dairy cases alongside fresh pasta and noodles. If you should have any pesto left over, I suggest using it within a few days or freezing it for later use.

2-CUP CAPACITY 12 SERVINGS	INGREDIENTS	3-CUP CAPACITY 16 SERVINGS
	YEAST	
1½ teaspoons	Active dry yeast	2¼ teaspoons
	DRY INGREDIENTS	
2 cups	Bread flour	3 cups
¾ teaspoon	Salt	1 teaspoon
1 teaspoon	Granulated white sugar	1½ teaspoons
	LIQUID INGREDIENTS	
½ cup, plus 2 tablespoons	Water	1 cup
3 tablespoons	Pesto	¼ cup
1 teaspoon	Lemon juice	1 teaspoon

All ingredients must be at room temperature, unless otherwise noted. Add ingredients in the order specified in your bread machine owner's manual. Set bread machine on the basic/standard bread making setting. Select medium or normal baking cycle. The programmable timer can be used, if desired.

Nutrition information per ½-inch slice:
132 calories, 3.09 g protein, 19.6 g carbohydrates, 0.76 g dietary fiber, 4.47 g fat, 2.28 mg cholesterol, 158 mg sodium, 35.4 mg potassium. Calories from protein: 9%; from carbohydrates: 60%; from fats: 31%.

HEARTY GRAIN AND HIGH-FIBER BREADS

STUDIES SHOW that we do not eat enough fiber. On average most Americans consume only 8 to 32 grams of dietary fiber a day, while people in Third World countries who suffer from much lower levels of coronary disease, diabetes, and other chronic illnesses, consume between 40 to 60 grams.

The bread recipes in this chapter were developed to contain between 1 to 2 grams of dietary fiber per ½-inch slice. Besides being good for you, they also taste wonderful and at least 66 to 85 percent of the calories in these breads are derived from carbohydrates, the majority of which come from complex carbohydrates, which are very low in fats and very high in nutritious vitamins.

For years we were made to believe that complex carbohydrates were fattening and should be avoided. We now know this is erroneous and that we must increase our intake of cereals and grains by at least three times in order to reduce the risk of chronic disease. Since it is advisable to increase the percentage of our caloric intake of total carbohydrates from an average of 46 percent to an average of between 55 and 61 percent, hearty grain and high-fiber breads look even more attractive now than ever before.

SEVEN-GRAIN MILLET BREAD

Back in the days when bread was made at home, bread baking was usually done once or twice a week and flour was milled at home by hand.

Today bread baking is much easier. Special mixtures of flour consisting of wheat, rye, oats, barley, soy, or triticale, to mention a few of the most popular grains, can be purchased at health food stores and through specialty catalogues. An expert miller's blend of the appropriate amount of each grain results in a delicious loaf of high-fiber bread.

Our seven-grain millet bread is rich in flavor and full of crunchy millet seeds, which are also available in health food stores and by mail from baking catalogues.

2-CUP CAPACITY 12 SERVINGS	INGREDIENTS	3-CUP CAPACITY 16 SERVINGS
	YEAST	
1½ teaspoons	Active dry yeast	2¼ teaspoons
	DRY INGREDIENTS	
1½ cups	Bread flour	2⅓ cups
½ cup	Seven-grain flour	⅔ cup
¼ cup	Lightly toasted millet seeds	⅓ cup
1 teaspoon	Salt	1½ teaspoons
2 tablespoons, plus 2 teaspoons	Nonfat dry milk	4 tablespoons
2 teaspoons	Unsalted butter or margarine	1 tablespoon
	LIQUID INGREDIENTS	
½ cup, plus 1 teaspoon	Water	¾ cup, plus 3 tablespoons
2 tablespoons	Honey	3 tablespoons
1 large	Egg	1 large
1 teaspoon	Lemon juice	1 teaspoon

All ingredients must be at room temperature, unless otherwise noted. Add ingredients in the order specified in your bread machine owner's manual. Set bread machine on the basic/standard bread making setting. Select medium or normal baking cycle. Do not use the programmable timer when making this bread since the recipe contains perishable ingredients.

Nutrition information per ½-inch slice:
108 calories, 3.53 g protein, 19.9 g carbohydrates, 0.91 g dietary fiber, 1.53 g fat, 19.6 mg cholesterol, 190 mg sodium, 96.8 mg potassium. Calories from protein: 13%; from carbohydrates: 74%; from fats: 13%.

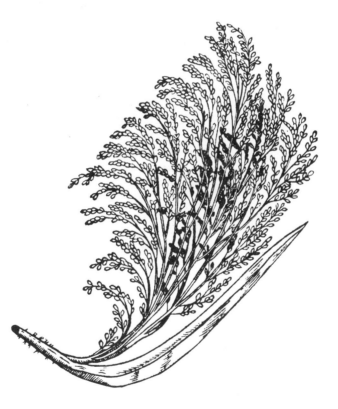

GOLDEN CRACKED WHEAT BREAD

As we all know, fiber is essential to a healthful diet. Wheat kernels are a virtual power-house of fiber, vitamins, and minerals. Two ½-inch slices of golden cracked wheat bread contain about 160 mg of potassium, or one tenth of the RDA.

Cracked wheat is the unprocessed wheat berry, or kernel, that has been crushed into pieces. Available in some specialty food and health food stores, the cracked wheat in this recipe adds texture and a warm golden hue to this bread.

2-CUP CAPACITY 12 SERVINGS	INGREDIENTS	3-CUP CAPACITY 16 SERVINGS
	YEAST	
1½ teaspoons	Active dry yeast	2¼ teaspoons
	DRY INGREDIENTS	
1½ cups	Bread flour	2¼ cups
½ cup	Whole-wheat flour	¾ cup
¼ cup	Cracked wheat	⅓ cup
1 teaspoon	Salt	1½ teaspoons
2 tablespoons, plus 2 teaspoons	Nonfat dry milk	4 tablespoons
2 teaspoons	Unsalted butter or margarine	1 tablespoon
	LIQUID INGREDIENTS	
½ cup, plus 1 tablespoon	Water	1 cup
2 tablespoons	Honey	3 tablespoons
1 large	Egg	1 large
1 teaspoon	Lemon juice	1 teaspoon

All ingredients must be at room temperature, unless otherwise noted. Add ingredients in the order specified in your bread machine owner's manual. Set bread machine on the basic/standard bread making setting. Select medium or normal baking cycle. Do not use the programmable timer when making this bread since the recipe contains perishable ingredients.

HINT: If dough appears too dry after kneading for the first couple of minutes, add additional water, no more than 1 tablespoon at a time, just until dough appears elastic. Do not add too much water.

Nutrition information per ½-inch slice:
111 calories, 3.64 g protein, 21.2 g carbohydrates, 1.80 g dietary fiber, 1.35 g fat, 19.6 mg cholesterol, 190 mg sodium, 78.4 mg potassium. Calories from protein: 13%; from carbohydrates: 76%; from fats: 11%.

BLACK BREAD

Black bread is peasant bread in its truest form. Traditionally made from heavier, unrefined flours and a sourdough starter, black bread has a very distinct flavor and texture.

In order to duplicate the true flavors of black bread in a bread machine it is necessary to be a bit creative. To get the bread to rise nicely, we have added bread flour along with the rye flour. Buttermilk gives the sourdough-like taste and the spices give the bread well-balanced flavor.

2-CUP CAPACITY 12 SERVINGS	INGREDIENTS	3-CUP CAPACITY 16 SERVINGS
	YEAST	
1½ teaspoons	Active dry yeast	2¼ teaspoons
	DRY INGREDIENTS	
1⅓ cups	Bread flour	2 cups
⅔ cup	Rye flour	1 cup
½ teaspoon	Caraway seeds	1 teaspoon
1 tablespoon	Coarsely ground cornmeal	1½ tablespoons
1 teaspoon	Instant coffee granules	1½ teaspoons
1 teaspoon	Unsweetened cocoa powder	1½ teaspoons
1 teaspoon	Onion powder	1½ teaspoons
1 teaspoon	Salt	1½ teaspoons
1 tablespoon	Dark brown sugar	1½ tablespoons
4 teaspoons	Unsalted butter or margarine	2 tablespoons
	LIQUID INGREDIENTS	
½ cup	Water	½ cup, plus 3 tablespoons
¼ cup, plus 2 tablespoons	Buttermilk	½ cup
1 tablespoon	Molasses	1½ tablespoons
1 teaspoon	Lemon juice	1 teaspoon

All ingredients must be at room temperature, unless otherwise noted. Add ingredients in the order specified in your bread machine owner's manual. Set bread machine on the basic/standard bread making setting. Select medium or normal baking cycle. Do not use the programmable timer when making this bread since the recipe contains perishable ingredients.

HINT: If dough appears too dry after kneading for the first couple of minutes, add additional water, no more than 1 tablespoon at a time, just until dough appears elastic. Do not add too much water.

Nutrition information per ½-inch slice:
97.9 calories, 2.46 g protein, 18.2 g carbohydrates, 1.42 g dietary fiber, 1.64 g fat, 3.73 mg cholesterol, 188 mg sodium, 80.8 mg potassium. Calories from protein: 10%; from carbohydrates: 75%; from fats: 15%.

SUNFLOWER WHEAT BREAD

There is nothing more beautiful than standing on top of a hill on my in-laws' farm and watching the swaying stalks of sunflowers stretch for miles and miles. The contrast of the deep blue sky and the bright yellow of the sunflowers inspired this wholesome bread scented with orange and full of nutty-tasting sunflower seeds.

2-CUP CAPACITY 12 SERVINGS	INGREDIENTS	3-CUP CAPACITY 16 SERVINGS
	YEAST	
1½ teaspoons	Active dry yeast	2¼ teaspoons
	DRY INGREDIENTS	
1¾ cups	Bread flour	2½ cups
¼ cup	Whole-wheat flour	½ cup
2 tablespoons	Medium rye flour	3 tablespoons
1½ teaspoons	Grated orange zest	2 teaspoons
1 teaspoon	Salt	1½ teaspoons
2 teaspoons	Granulated white sugar	1 tablespoon
2 tablespoons, plus 1 teaspoon	Nonfat dry milk	4 tablespoons
2 teaspoons	Unsalted butter or margarine	1 tablespoon
	LIQUID INGREDIENTS	
¾ cup, plus 2 teaspoons	Water	1¼ cups, plus 1 tablespoon
1 teaspoon	Lemon juice	1 teaspoon
	SUNFLOWER SEEDS	
¼ cup	Unsalted, shelled sunflower seeds	⅓ cup

All ingredients must be at room temperature, unless otherwise noted. Add ingredients in the order specified in your bread machine owner's manual. Add **sunflower seeds** at the appropriate moment for your model bread machine. Set bread machine on the basic/standard bread making setting. Select medium or normal baking cycle. The programmable timer can be used, if desired.

Nutrition information per ½-inch slice:
99.7 calories, 3.08 g protein, 16.5 g carbohydrates, 0.97 g dietary fiber, 2.34 g fat, 1.87 mg cholesterol, 183 mg sodium, 65 mg potassium. Calories from protein: 13%; from carbohydrates: 66%; from fats: 21%.

APPLE WHEAT BREAD

The tart juice of the apple adds extra moistness and flavor to this testimony to autumn.

2-CUP CAPACITY	INGREDIENTS	3-CUP CAPACITY
12 SERVINGS		**16 SERVINGS**
	YEAST	
1½ teaspoons	Active dry yeast	2¼ teaspoons
	DRY INGREDIENTS	
1¾ cups	Bread flour	2⅔ cups
¼ cup	Whole-wheat flour	⅓ cup
¾ teaspoon	Ground cinnamon	1 teaspoon
2 pinches	Ground nutmeg	¼ teaspoon
1 teaspoon	Salt	1½ teaspoons
4 teaspoons	Dark brown sugar	2 tablespoons
2 tablespoons, plus 2 teaspoons	Nonfat dry milk	4 tablespoons
2 teaspoons	Unsalted butter or margarine	1 tablespoon
	LIQUID INGREDIENTS	
½ cup, less 1 tablespoon	Water	½ cup, plus 3 tablespoons
½ cup	Coarsely chopped, peeled, tart apple	¾ cup
1 teaspoon	Lemon juice	1 teaspoon

All ingredients must be at room temperature, unless otherwise noted. Add ingredients in the order specified in your bread machine owner's manual. Set bread machine on the basic/standard bread making setting. Select medium or normal baking cycle. The programmable timer can be used, if desired.

HINT: If dough appears too dry after kneading for the first couple of minutes, add additional water, no more than 1 tablespoon at a time, just until dough appears elastic. Do not add too much water.

Nutrition information per ½-inch slice:
89.2 calories, 2.69 g protein, 18.8 g carbohydrates, 1.09 g dietary fiber, 0.28 g fat, 0.16 mg cholesterol, 184 mg sodium, 64.7 mg potassium. Calories from protein: 12%; from carbohydrates: 85%; from fats: 3%.

ANADAMA BREAD

This New England bread has a story behind its name.

A New England farmer had a lazy wife named Anna who would serve him the same tiresome dish of cornmeal porridge every day. One day he became disgusted and decided to take matters into his own hands. He began adding whatever he could find in the kitchen to his porridge: some flour, some mead, and some molasses. He then shaped it into a loaf and threw it on the fire. When he finally tasted his creation he decided he could easily get through life without his good-for-nothing wife, and exclaimed, "Anna, damn her!"

2-CUP CAPACITY 12 SERVINGS	INGREDIENTS	3-CUP CAPACITY 16 SERVINGS
	YEAST	
1½ teaspoons	Active dry yeast	2¼ teaspoons
	DRY INGREDIENTS	
1¾ cups	Bread flour	2½ cups
¼ cup	Whole-wheat flour	½ cup
¼ cup	Coarsely ground cornmeal	⅓ cup
1 teaspoon	Salt	1½ teaspoons
2 tablespoons, plus 2 teaspoons	Nonfat dry milk	4 tablespoons
4 teaspoons	Unsalted butter or margarine	2 tablespoons
	LIQUID INGREDIENTS	
¾ cup, plus 1 tablespoon	Water	1¼ cups
2 tablespoons	Molasses	3 tablespoons
1 teaspoon	Lemon juice	1 teaspoon

All ingredients must be at room temperature, unless otherwise noted. Add ingredients in the order specified in your bread machine owner's manual. Set bread machine on the basic/standard bread making setting. Select medium or normal baking cycle. Do not use the programmable timer when making this bread since the recipe contains ingredients that can absorb the water prior to the start of the bread making process.

HINT: If dough appears too dry after kneading for the first couple of minutes, add additional water, no more than 1 tablespoon at a time, just until dough appears elastic. Do not add too much water.

Nutrition information per ½-inch slice:
96.7 calories, 2.91 g protein, 20.3 g carbohydrates, 1.21 g dietary fiber, 0.29 g fat, 0.167 mg cholesterol, 185 mg sodium, 87.3 mg potassium. Calories from protein: 12%; from carbohydrates: 85%; from fats: 3%.

SEMOLINA SESAME BREAD

Semolina is flour milled from hard durum wheat, and is sometimes used in pasta and noodles. This intensely yellow flour is too coarsely ground to be used for making bread and has to be mixed with bread flour.

Thanks to the addition of toasted sesame seeds, semolina sesame bread is a nutty-tasting bread with a crisp crust and fluffy crumb, just like a good loaf of Italian bread.

2-CUP CAPACITY 12 Servings	INGREDIENTS	3-CUP CAPACITY 16 Servings
	YEAST	
1½ teaspoons	Active dry yeast	2¼ teaspoons
	DRY INGREDIENTS	
1½ cups	Bread flour	2⅓ cups
½ cup	Semolina flour	⅔ cup
1 teaspoon	Salt	1½ teaspoons
1 teaspoon	Granulated white sugar	1½ teaspoons
4 teaspoons	Nonfat dry milk	2 tablespoons
1 teaspoon	Unsalted butter or margarine	1½ teaspoons
	LIQUID INGREDIENTS	
½ cup, plus 2 tablespoons	Water	1 cup
1 large	Egg	1 large
1 teaspoon	Lemon juice	1 teaspoon
	SESAME SEEDS	
¼ cup	Lightly toasted sesame seeds	⅓ cup

All ingredients must be at room temperature, unless otherwise noted. Add ingredients in the order specified in your bread machine owner's manual. Set bread machine on the basic/standard bread making setting. Add **sesame seeds** at the appropriate moment for your model bread machine. Select medium or normal baking cycle. Do not use the programmable timer when making this bread since the recipe contains perishable ingredients.

Nutrition information per ½-inch slice:
112 calories, 3.83 g protein, 18.4 g carbohydrates, 1.05 g dietary fiber, 2.46 g fat, 18.7 mg cholesterol, 97.8 mg sodium, 63.2 mg potassium. Calories from protein: 14%; from carbohydrates: 66%; from fats: 20%.

MOLASSES OAT BREAD

When refined white sugar was more expensive than molasses, those who could not afford sugar would use molasses for their sweetening needs. Little did they know that molasses, the syrup that remains after making white sugar, is rich in iron, calcium, and phosphorus. Molasses, combined with oats, gives this bread its moisture, unique texture, and taste.

2-CUP CAPACITY 12 SERVINGS	INGREDIENTS	3-CUP CAPACITY 16 SERVINGS
	YEAST	
1½ teaspoons	Active dry yeast	2¼ teaspoons
	DRY INGREDIENTS	
2 cups	Bread flour	3 cups
⅓ cup	Rolled oats	½ cup
1 teaspoon	Salt	1½ teaspoons
2 teaspoons	Dark brown sugar	1 tablespoon
4 teaspoons	Nonfat dry milk	2 tablespoons
2 teaspoons	Unsalted butter or margarine	1 tablespoon
	LIQUID INGREDIENTS	
¾ cup, plus 1 teaspoon	Water	1 cup, plus 2 tablespoons
4 teaspoons	Molasses	2 tablespoons
1 teaspoon	Lemon juice	1 teaspoon

All ingredients must be at room temperature, unless otherwise noted. Add ingredients in the order specified in your bread machine owner's manual. Set bread machine on the basic/standard bread making setting. Select medium or normal baking cycle except for Panasonic/National models, which should be set on light. Do not use the programmable timer when making this bread since the recipe contains ingredients that can absorb the water prior to the start of the bread making process.

HINT: If dough appears too dry after kneading for the first couple of minutes, add additional water, no more than 1 tablespoon at a time, just until dough appears elastic. Do not add too much water.

Nutrition information per ½-inch slice:
100 calories, 2.79 g protein, 19.6 g carbohydrates, 0.90 g dietary fiber, 0.99 g fat, 1.81 mg cholesterol, 182 mg sodium, 67.7 mg potassium. Calories from protein: 11%; from carbohydrates: 80%; from fats: 9%.

HEARTLAND RAISIN NUT BREAD

Near the end of the eighteenth century a Swiss physician, Dr. Bircher-Benner, developed a nutritious mixture of dried fruits, milk, grains, and nuts that he called muesli. The forerunner of today's granola, muesli provides the best ingredients from the heartland to start the day off right.

Heartland raisin nut bread is chock full of all the ingredients Dr. Bircher-Benner recommended.

2-CUP CAPACITY 12 SERVINGS	INGREDIENTS	3-CUP CAPACITY 16 SERVINGS
	YEAST	
1½ teaspoons	Active dry yeast	2¼ teaspoons
	DRY INGREDIENTS	
1¾ cups	Bread flour	2½ cups
¼ cup	Whole-wheat flour	½ cup
2 tablespoons	Toasted wheat germ	3 tablespoons
1 teaspoon	Salt	1½ teaspoons
2 teaspoons	Dark brown sugar	1 tablespoon
2 tablespoons, plus 1 teaspoon	Nonfat dry milk	4 tablespoons
2 teaspoons	Unsalted butter or margarine	1 tablespoon
	LIQUID INGREDIENTS	
¾ cup	Water	1 cup, plus 2 tablespoons
1 large	Egg	1 large
1 teaspoon	Lemon juice	1 teaspoon
	FRUIT AND NUTS	
2 tablespoons	Dark raisins	3 tablespoons
2 tablespoons	Golden raisins	3 tablespoons
¼ cup	Chopped, toasted walnuts	⅓ cup

All ingredients must be at room temperature, unless otherwise noted. Add ingredients in the order specified in your bread machine owner's manual. Add **fruit and nuts** at the appropriate moment for your model bread machine. Set bread machine on the basic/standard bread making setting. Select medium or normal baking cycle. Do not use the programmable timer when making this bread since the recipe contains perishable ingredients.

HINT: If dough appears too dry after kneading for the first couple of minutes, add additional water, no more than 1 tablespoon at a time, just until dough appears elastic. Do not add too much water.

Nutrition information per ½-inch slice:
124 calories, 3.96 g protein, 20.6 g carbohydrates, 1.45 g dietary fiber, 2.98 g fat, 19.6 mg cholesterol, 189 mg sodium, 106 mg potassium. Calories from protein: 13%; from carbohydrates: 66%; from fats: 21%.

GROOM'S BREAD

Wedding cakes of years gone by were very different from the ones we know today. Up until the late 1800s, wedding cakes were a type of iced fruit cake, heavy on the spices and rum. As the three-tier layer cake came into fashion, the fruit cake-style wedding cake became known as the groom's cake.

Groom's bread is so called because it is also dense and dark, and full of dried fruits like apples, pears, peaches, and prunes. Because the bread is dense, slice very thin.

2-CUP CAPACITY 12 SERVINGS	INGREDIENTS	3-CUP CAPACITY 16 SERVINGS
	YEAST	
1½ teaspoons	Active dry yeast	2¼ teaspoons
	DRY INGREDIENTS	
1¾ cups	Bread flour	2½ cups
¼ cup	Whole-wheat flour	½ cup
¼ cup	Toasted wheat germ	⅓ cup
2 teaspoons	Grated orange zest	1 tablespoon
1 teaspoon	Salt	1½ teaspoons
4 teaspoons	Dark brown sugar	2 tablespoons
2 tablespoons, plus 1 teaspoon	Nonfat dry milk	4 tablespoons
4 teaspoons	Unsalted butter or margarine	2 tablespoons
	LIQUID INGREDIENTS	
¾ cup, plus 2 tablespoons	Water	1¼ cups, plus 1 tablespoon
	FRUIT	
⅓ cup	Coarsely chopped, mixed dried fruits	½ cup

All ingredients must be at room temperature, unless otherwise noted. Add ingredients in the order specified in your bread machine owner's manual. Add **fruit** at the appropriate moment for your model bread machine. Set bread machine on the basic/standard bread making setting. Select medium or normal baking cycle. Do not use the programmable timer when making this bread since the recipe contains ingredients that can absorb the water prior to the start of the bread making process.

Hint: If dough appears too dry after kneading for the first couple of minutes, add additional water, no more than 1 tablespoon at a time, just until dough appears elastic. Do not add too much water.

Nutrition information per ½-inch slice:
149 calories, 3.95 g protein, 30.0 g carbohydrates, 1.93 g dietary fiber, 1.86 g fat, 3.60 mg cholesterol, 187 mg sodium, 194 mg potassium. Calories from protein: 10%; from carbohydrates: 79%; from fats: 11%.

HONEY NUT WHEAT BREAD

There has been a lot of talk lately about the cholesterol-reducing properties of walnuts. Only time will tell whether there is any validity in such reports. Nevertheless, chopped, toasted walnuts are a welcome taste addition to wheat bread when added along with toasted wheat germ.

2-CUP CAPACITY 12 SERVINGS	INGREDIENTS	3-CUP CAPACITY 16 SERVINGS
	YEAST	
1½ teaspoons	Active dry yeast	2¼ teaspoons
	DRY INGREDIENTS	
1¾ cups	Bread flour	2⅔ cups
¼ cup	Whole-wheat flour	⅓ cup
2 tablespoons	Toasted wheat germ	3 tablespoons
1 teaspoon	Salt	1½ teaspoons
2 tablespoons, plus 2 teaspoons	Nonfat dry milk	4 tablespoons
2 teaspoons	Unsalted butter or margarine	1 tablespoon
	LIQUID INGREDIENTS	
¾ cup, plus 1 tablespoon	Water	1 cup, plus 1 tablespoon
3 tablespoons	Honey	¼ cup
1 teaspoon	Lemon juice	1 teaspoon
	NUTS	
⅓ cup	Chopped, toasted walnuts	½ cup

All ingredients must be at room temperature, unless otherwise noted. Add ingredients in the order specified in your bread machine owner's manual. Add **nuts** at the appropriate moment for your model bread machine. Set bread machine on the basic/standard bread making setting. Select medium or normal baking cycle except for Panasonic/National models, which should be set on light. Do not use the programmable timer when making this bread since the recipe contains ingredients that can absorb the water prior to the start of the bread making process.

HINT: If dough appears too dry after kneading for the first couple of minutes, add additional water, no more than 1 tablespoon at a time, just until dough appears elastic. Do not add too much water.

Nutrition information per ½-inch slice:
126 calories, 3.50 g protein, 21.8 g carbohydrates, 1.26 g dietary fiber, 3.04 g fat, 1.89 mg cholesterol, 185 mg sodium, 82.7 mg potassium. Calories from protein: 11%; from carbohydrates: 68%; from fats: 21%.

HONEY GRAHAM GRANOLA BREAD

Granola cereal adds an interesting crunch to this bread. For best results, use either homemade granola or a store-bought brand that is low in fat and sugar.

Since there are so many different types of granola, the amount of water required in the recipe may vary. Check the dough during the first kneading cycle to make sure it is not too dry.

2-CUP CAPACITY 12 SERVINGS	INGREDIENTS	3-CUP CAPACITY 16 SERVINGS
	YEAST	
1½ teaspoons	Active dry yeast	2¼ teaspoons
	DRY INGREDIENTS	
1¾ cups	Bread flour	2⅔ cups
¼ cup	Whole-wheat flour	⅓ cup
⅓ cup	Granola cereal	½ cup
1 teaspoon	Salt	1½ teaspoons
2 tablespoons, plus 2 teaspoons	Nonfat dry milk	4 tablespoons
2 teaspoons	Unsalted butter or margarine	1 tablespoon
	LIQUID INGREDIENTS	
¾ cup, plus 2 tablespoons	Water	1¼ cups
3 tablespoons	Honey	¼ cup
1 teaspoon	Lemon juice	1 teaspoon

All ingredients must be at room temperature, unless otherwise noted. Add ingredients in the order specified in your bread machine owner's manual. Set bread machine on the basic/standard bread making setting. If possible, select light baking cycle. If not, use medium or normal setting. Do not use the programmable timer when making this bread since the recipe contains ingredients that can absorb the water prior to the start of the bread making process.

Golden Cracked-Wheat Bread (page 48)

Black Bread (page 50)

Apple Wheat Bread (page 53)

Honey Graham Granola Bread (page 64)

Heartland Raisin Nut Bread (page 58)

Molasses Oat Bread (page 57)

Sweet Potato Pecan Bread (page 70)

HINT: If dough appears too dry after kneading for the first couple of minutes, add additional water, no more than 1 tablespoon at a time, just until dough appears elastic. Do not add too much water.

Nutrition information per ½-inch slice:
105 calories, 3.09 g protein, 19.1 g carbohydrates, 1.26 g dietary fiber, 1.79 g fat, 1.89 mg cholesterol, 184 mg sodium, 69.8 mg potassium. Calories from protein: 12%; from carbohydrates: 73%; from fats: 15%.

Cardamom Golden Raisin Almond Bread (page 74)

FIG WALNUT WHEAT BREAD

If you have ever eaten a fresh fig you can easily understand why they were held sacred by the ancients. Pleasantly sweet with a mixture of textures in every bite, figs are highly perishable. Fortunately, figs dry very well and are readily available in all supermarkets year round. Dried figs are also high in iron, calcium, and phosphorus.

Fig walnut wheat bread is an adaptation of a nonyeast fig bread from Spain called *pan de higo*. This bread should be sliced very thin when served.

2-CUP CAPACITY 12 SERVINGS	INGREDIENTS	3-CUP CAPACITY 16 SERVINGS
	YEAST	
1½ teaspoons	Active dry yeast	2½ teaspoons
	DRY INGREDIENTS	
2 cups	Bread flour	3 cups
¼ cup	Toasted wheat germ	⅓ cup
1 teaspoon	Unsweetened cocoa powder	1½ teaspoons
½ teaspoon	Ground cinnamon	¾ teaspoon
¾ teaspoon	Salt	1 teaspoon
2 tablespoons, plus 2 teaspoons	Nonfat dry milk	4 tablespoons
2 teaspoons	Unsalted butter or margarine	1 tablespoon
	LIQUID INGREDIENTS	
¾ cup, plus 2 tablespoons	Water	1 cup, plus 3 tablespoons
2 tablespoons	Honey	3 tablespoons
	FRUIT AND NUTS	
⅓ cup	Coarsely chopped dried Calimyrna figs	½ cup
¼ cup	Toasted, chopped walnuts	⅓ cup

All ingredients must be at room temperature, unless otherwise noted. Add ingredients in the order specified in your bread machine owner's manual. Set bread machine on the basic/standard bread making setting. Add **fruit and nuts** at the appropriate moment for your model bread machine. Select medium or normal baking cycle. Do not use the programmable timer when making this bread since the recipe contains ingredients that can absorb the water prior to the start of the bread making process.

Hint: If dough appears too dry after kneading for the first couple of minutes, add additional water, no more than 1 tablespoon at a time, just until dough appears elastic. Do not add too much water.

Nutrition information per ½-inch slice:
128 calories, 3.76 g protein, 22.6 g carbohydrates, 1.46 g dietary fiber, 2.71 g fat, 1.89 mg cholesterol, 140 mg sodium, 100 mg potassium. Calories from protein: 11%; from carbohydrates: 70%; from fats: 19%.

Old-Fashioned Country and Celebration Breads

AMERICA HAS ALWAYS had a strong tradition of home baking. Up until the late 1800s, most baked goods were prepared at home, and most commonly it was the female head of the household who had to be well versed in all aspects of bread baking. Envisioning these old-fashioned breads, one conjures up images of freshly baked loaves with a wonderfully homespun, slightly imperfect appearance and with steam gently rising from a warm slice. Just one bite of this dreamy slice would tell you how much time and love went into the kneading and baking of this bread.

Each family had its favorite recipes, which were passed on from generation to generation, and these recipes often reflected characteristics particular to the baker's region and time period in which she lived. Following many years of decline, home bread baking has entered a period of renewed interest. New breads and variations have appeared in the past few years which mirror the time in which we live, inspired more by creative and dietary considerations than by what ingredients are most readily available.

Bread has always been a part of family traditions and celebrations around the world, with certain breads being served for specific holidays or festivals. While most of these breads are hand-shaped, the celebration bread recipes in this chapter can easily be made and baked in your bread machine, to enjoy for special occasions or any day of the year.

SWEET POTATO PECAN BREAD

The first time I had this native bread of Mississippi, I could not figure out what gave it its deep rich color and moist texture. I was very surprised to later learn that it was sweet potato.

Beta-carotene, the form of vitamin A found in orange and dark green vegetables, is an essential vitamin in a well-balanced diet, acting as a protector to our immune system against disease. In fact, two slices of sweet potato pecan bread provide approximately 20 percent of the RDA of this very important vitamin.

Allow extra time when making this bread to prepare the mashed sweet potatoes.

2-CUP CAPACITY 12 SERVINGS	INGREDIENTS	3-CUP CAPACITY 16 SERVINGS
	YEAST	
1½ teaspoons	Active dry yeast	2¼ teaspoons
	DRY INGREDIENTS	
2 cups	Bread flour	3 cups
3 tablespoons	Rolled oats	4 tablespoons
¼ teaspoon	Ground cinnamon	½ teaspoon
1 pinch	Ground nutmeg	2 pinches
1 teaspoon	Salt	1½ teaspoons
4 teaspoons	Dark brown sugar	2 tablespoons
2 tablespoons	Nonfat dry milk	3 tablespoons
2 tablespoons	Unsalted butter or margarine	3 tablespoons
	LIQUID INGREDIENTS	
½ cup	Plain, mashed sweet potatoes (see note)	¾ cup
½ cup	Water	¾ cup
	FRUIT AND NUTS	
2 tablespoons	Dark raisins	3 tablespoons
¼ cup	Chopped pecans	⅓ cup

All ingredients must be at room temperature, unless otherwise noted. Add ingredients in the order specified in your bread machine owner's manual. Set bread machine on the basic/standard bread making setting. Add **fruit and nuts** at the appropriate moment for your model bread machine. Select medium or normal baking cycle. The programmable timer can be used, if desired.

HINT: If dough appears too dry after kneading for the first couple of minutes, add additional water, no more than 1 tablespoon at a time, just until dough appears elastic. Do not add too much water.

NOTE: To make mashed sweet potatoes, for 2-cup-capacity recipe, bake an 8-ounce sweet potato in a 400° oven for approximately 1 hour, or until tender. Remove from oven. Cut in half and remove potato from skin. Mash in a small bowl until smooth. Cool to room temperature before using. For 3-cup-capacity recipe, bake two 6-ounce sweet potatoes. Follow same procedure.

Nutrition information per ½-inch slice:
138 calories, 3.15 g protein, 22.5 g carbohydrates, 1.29 g dietary fiber, 3.92 g fat, 5.30 mg cholesterol, 189 mg sodium, 106 mg potassium. Calories from protein: 9%; from carbohydrates: 65%; from fats: 26%.

LEMON POPPY SEED BREAD

Lemon and poppy seeds make an interesting flavor combination. Usually combined in a bundt cake, they also work well together in this sweet bread with a light lemon glaze which you can make while the bread is cooling.

2-CUP CAPACITY 12 SERVINGS	INGREDIENTS	3-CUP CAPACITY 16 SERVINGS
	YEAST	
1½ teaspoons	Active dry yeast	2¼ teaspoons
	DRY INGREDIENTS	
2 cups	Bread flour	3 cups
2 teaspoons	Grated lemon zest	1 tablespoon
1 teaspoon	Poppy seeds	1½ teaspoons
¾ teaspoon	Salt	1 teaspoon
4 teaspoons	Granulated white sugar	2 tablespoons
2 tablespoons, plus 1 teaspoon	Nonfat dry milk	4 tablespoons
2 teaspoons	Unsalted butter or margarine	1 tablespoon
	LIQUID INGREDIENTS	
½ cup	Water	1 cup
1 large	Egg	1 large
1 teaspoon	Lemon juice	1 teaspoon
	LEMON GLAZE	
2 teaspoons	Unsalted butter or margarine, softened	
1 teaspoon	Grated lemon zest	
4 tablespoons	Confectioners' sugar	
1–2 teaspoons	Lemon juice	

All ingredients must be at room temperature, unless otherwise noted. Add ingredients, except those for lemon glaze, in the order specified in your bread machine owner's manual. Set bread machine on the basic/standard bread making setting. If possible, select light baking cycle. If not, use medium or normal setting. Do not use the programmable timer when making this bread since the recipe contains perishable ingredients.

While the baked bread cools to room temperature, make the glaze. Cream butter or margarine with grated lemon zest and confectioners' sugar. Gradually add lemon juice until smooth and thin enough to drizzle. Glaze cooled loaf of bread by drizzling glaze on top and sides of loaf. Let dry before slicing. Yield: enough glaze for one loaf.

Nutrition information per ½-inch slice:
109 calories, 3.39 g protein, 20.2 g carbohydrates, 0.79 g dietary fiber, 1.40 g fat, 15.4 mg cholesterol, 144 mg sodium, 58.1 mg potassium. Calories from protein: 13%; from carbohydrates: 75%; from fats: 12%.

CARDAMOM GOLDEN RAISIN ALMOND BREAD

Cardamom is a very fragrant, flavorful spice that adds a spicy-sweet flavor to baked goods. It is a popular ingredient in Scandinavian breads, cookies, and cakes.

Cardamom golden raisin almond bread is a variation of a Danish sweet bread I once received as a gift. It is rich in butter, eggs, and cardamom. Sprinkled with a dusting of confectioners' sugar, the loaf is also attractive when sliced, since it is chock full of golden raisins and almonds.

2-CUP CAPACITY 12 SERVINGS	INGREDIENTS	3-CUP CAPACITY 16 SERVINGS
	YEAST	
1½ teaspoons	Active dry yeast	2¼ teaspoons
	DRY INGREDIENTS	
2 cups	Bread flour	3 cups
½ teaspoon	Ground cardamom	¾ teaspoon
¾ teaspoon	Salt	1 teaspoon
4 teaspoons	Granulated white sugar	2 tablespoons
2 tablespoons, plus 1 teaspoon	Nonfat dry milk	4 tablespoons
2 teaspoons	Unsalted butter or margarine	1 tablespoon
	LIQUID INGREDIENTS	
½ cup	Water	¾ cup, plus 3 tablespoons
1 teaspoon	Vanilla extract	1½ teaspoons
1 large	Egg	1 large
1 teaspoon	Lemon juice	1 teaspoon
	FRUIT AND NUTS	
⅓ cup	Golden raisins	½ cup
⅓ cup	Slivered almonds	½ cup
	FOR DUSTING	
	Confectioners' sugar	

All ingredients must be at room temperature, unless otherwise noted. Add ingredients in the order specified in your bread machine owner's manual. Add **fruit and nuts** at the appropriate moment for your model bread machine. Set bread machine on the basic/standard bread making setting. If possible, select light baking cycle. If not, use medium or normal setting. Do not use the programmable timer when making this bread since the recipe contains perishable ingredients. If desired, dust bread with confectioners' sugar after bread has cooled to room temperature.

Nutrition information per ½-inch slice:
132 calories, 3.97 g protein, 22.1 g carbohydrates, 1.48 g dietary fiber, 3.23 g fat, 19.6 mg cholesterol, 145 mg sodium, 109 mg potassium. Calories from protein: 12%; from carbohydrates: 66%; from fats: 22%.

made March 13, 2015 — needs more cardamom! I used whole ones. Set machine on light.

ORANGE CRANBERRY NUT BREAD

Almost addictive, the sweet-and-sour taste of these dried cranberries is great for using in place of raisins in all types of baked goods.

Very high in vitamin C, cranberries mix well with oranges. The sweet and slightly tart taste of orange cranberry nut bread will certainly make it a favorite in your home.

2-CUP CAPACITY 12 SERVINGS	INGREDIENTS	3-CUP CAPACITY 16 SERVINGS
	YEAST	
1½ teaspoons	Active dry yeast	2¼ teaspoons
	DRY INGREDIENTS	
2 cups	Bread flour	3 cups
2 teaspoons	Grated orange zest	1 tablespoon
¾ teaspoon	Salt	1 teaspoon
4 teaspoons	Granulated white sugar	2 tablespoons
2 tablespoons, plus 1 teaspoon	Nonfat dry milk	4 tablespoons
2 teaspoons	Unsalted butter or margarine	1 tablespoon
	LIQUID INGREDIENTS	
½ cup	Water	1 cup
1 large	Egg	1 large
1 teaspoon	Vanilla extract	1½ teaspoons
1 teaspoon	Lemon juice	1 teaspoon
	FRUIT AND NUTS	
⅓ cup	Dried, sweetened cranberries	½ cup
⅓ cup	Chopped, toasted walnuts	½ cup

All ingredients must be at room temperature, unless otherwise noted. Add ingredients in the order specified in your bread machine owner's manual. Add **fruit and nuts** at the appropriate moment for your model bread machine. Set bread machine on the basic/standard bread making setting. If possible, select light baking cycle. If not, use medium or normal setting. Do not use the programmable timer when making this bread since the recipe contains perishable ingredients.

Nutrition information per ½-inch slice:
145 calories, 4.02 g protein, 24.5 g carbohydrates, 1.26 g dietary fiber, 3.62 g fat, 15.4 mg cholesterol, 145 mg sodium, 109 mg potassium. Calories from protein: 11%; from carbohydrates: 67%; from fats: 22%.

CINNAMON COFFEE BREAD

The trick to this bread is knowing when to add the frozen streusel filling. The key is to determine whether your bread machine has a special program for adding raisins, nuts, etc. If so, add the filling at that moment. If not, add the filling 5 minutes before the end of the final kneading.

In the event that the streusel filling does not blend into the dough, remove the dough from the pan and, on a lightly floured work surface, knead the dough to help spread the filling. Put the dough back into bread machine pan immediately after spreading streusel filling, lower lid and let the dough continue rising.

Allow extra time when making this bread to prepare the streusel filling. Filling should be frozen for at least 2 hours before using.

2-CUP CAPACITY 12 SERVINGS	INGREDIENTS	3-CUP CAPACITY 16 SERVINGS
	YEAST	
1½ teaspoons	Active dry yeast	2¼ teaspoons
	DRY INGREDIENTS	
2 cups	Bread flour	3 cups
¾ teaspoon	Salt	1 teaspoon
2 teaspoons	Granulated white sugar	1 tablespoon
2 tablespoons, plus 1 teaspoon	Nonfat dry milk	4 tablespoons
1 teaspoon	Unsalted butter or margarine	1½ teaspoons
	LIQUID INGREDIENTS	
½ cup	Water	1 cup
1 large	Egg	1 large
1 teaspoon	Lemon juice	1 teaspoon
	FILLING	
1½ tablespoons	Unsalted butter or margarine	2 tablespoons
2½ tablespoons	Dark brown sugar	3 tablespoons
1 teaspoon	Ground cinnamon	1½ teaspoons
¼ cup	Chopped walnuts	⅓ cup
1 tablespoon	Bread flour	1½ tablespoons

All ingredients must be at room temperature, unless otherwise noted. Add ingredients in the order specified in your bread machine owner's manual. Add **streusel filling** at the appropriate moment for your model bread machine. Set bread machine on the basic/standard bread making setting. Select medium or normal baking cycle. Do not use the programmable timer when making this bread since the recipe contains perishable ingredients.

To prepare the streusel filling, mix together all ingredients except for bread flour. Place on a piece of plastic wrap and shape into a cylinder approximately 2 inches in diameter. Wrap well. Freeze until solid, approximately two hours. Do not remove from freezer until ready to use. Cut into ¼-inch cubes with very sharp knife. Sprinkle with the bread flour to coat so that streusel cubes do not stick together. Refreeze any leftover streusel filling.

Nutrition information per ½-inch slice:
145 calories, 3.65 g protein, 21.7 g carbohydrates, 0.94 g dietary fiber, 4.93 g fat, 23.9 mg cholesterol, 146 mg sodium, 79.0 mg potassium. Calories from protein: 10%; from carbohydrates: 60%; from fats: 30%.

Greek Christopsomo Anise Bread

Christopsomo is a traditional Greek Christmas bread made with crushed anise seeds or *mastîhi*, a dried pine resin available in some Middle East specialty food stores. The bread is usually baked in large rounds on top of which the baker sculpts religious symbols and flowers from leftover dough.

This bread is equally good baked in a bread machine. Serve as a light dessert with fresh fruit and coffee or lightly toasted in the morning for breakfast.

2-CUP CAPACITY 12 SERVINGS	INGREDIENTS	3-CUP CAPACITY 16 SERVINGS
	YEAST	
1½ teaspoons	Active dry yeast	2¼ teaspoons
	DRY INGREDIENTS	
2 cups	Bread flour	3 cups
¾ teaspoon	Crushed anise seed	1 teaspoon
½ teaspoon	Salt	¾ teaspoon
3 tablespoons	Granulated white sugar	4 tablespoons
2 tablespoons, plus 1 teaspoon	Nonfat dry milk	4 tablespoons
2 tablespoons	Unsalted butter or margarine	3 tablespoons
	LIQUID INGREDIENTS	
½ cup, plus 1 tablespoon	Water	¾ cup
1 large	Egg	2 large
1 teaspoon	Lemon juice	1 teaspoon
ANISE GLAZE		
1 cup	Confectioners' sugar	
½ teaspoon	Anise extract	
3–4 teaspoons	Water	

All ingredients must be at room temperature, unless otherwise noted. Add ingredients in the order specified in your bread machine owner's manual. Set bread machine on the basic/standard bread making setting. If possible, select light baking cycle. If not, use medium or normal setting. Do not use the programmable timer when making this bread since the recipe contains perishable ingredients.

While baked bread cools to room temperature, make glaze. Gradually add anise extract and water to confectioners' sugar until smooth and thin enough to drizzle. Glaze cooled loaf of bread by drizzling glaze on tops and sides of loaf. Let dry before slicing. Yield: enough glaze for one loaf.

Nutrition information per ½-inch slice:
115 calories, 3.09 g protein, 19.5 g carbohydrates, 0.66 g dietary fiber, 2.55 g fat,
23.1 mg cholesterol, 99.7 mg sodium, 48.5 mg potassium. Calories from protein: 11%;
from carbohydrates: 69%; from fats: 20%.

MORAVIAN LOVEFEAST BREAD

The Moravian Church is a Protestant sect originally established in Central Europe. The lovefeast ceremony is a traditional part of the Moravian faith, celebrating the birth of Christ.

Moravian lovefeast bread is traditionally made in the shape of sweet rolls and served after church services on Christmas Eve. This wonderfully sweet bread, with its enticing aroma and taste of oranges and spices, is great for breakfast or coffee.

Allow extra time when making this bread to prepare the mashed potatoes.

2-CUP CAPACITY 12 SERVINGS	INGREDIENTS	3-CUP CAPACITY 16 SERVINGS
	YEAST	
1½ teaspoons	Active dry yeast	2¼ teaspoons
	DRY INGREDIENTS	
2 cups	Bread flour	3 cups
2 teaspoons	Grated orange zest	1 tablespoon
1 pinch	Ground nutmeg	2 pinches
1 pinch	Ground mace	2 pinches
¾ teaspoon	Salt	1 teaspoon
2½ tablespoons	Granulated white sugar	4 tablespoons
4 teaspoons	Nonfat dry milk	2 tablespoons
4 teaspoons	Unsalted butter or margarine	2 tablespoons
	LIQUID INGREDIENTS	
⅓ cup	Plain, mashed potatoes (see note)	½ cup
⅓ cup, plus 1 teaspoon	Water	½ cup, plus 2 tablespoons
2 teaspoons	Freshly squeezed orange juice	1 tablespoon
1 large	Egg	1 large

All ingredients must be at room temperature, unless otherwise noted. Add ingredients in the order specified in your bread machine owner's manual. Set bread machine on the basic/standard bread making setting. If possible, select light baking cycle. If not, use medium or normal setting. Do not use the programmable timer when making this bread since the recipe contains perishable ingredients.

HINT: If dough appears too dry after kneading for the first couple of minutes, add additional water, no more than 1 tablespoon at a time, just until dough appears elastic. Do not add too much water.

NOTE: To make mashed potatoes, for 2-cup-capacity recipe, peel and quarter a medium 4-ounce red potato. Boil until tender in unsalted water. Drain well. Mash potato with a fork until smooth. Cool to room temperature before using. For 3-cup-capacity recipe, peel and quarter a large 6-ounce red potato. Follow same procedure.

Nutrition information per ½-inch slice:
111 calories, 3.09 g protein, 20.0 g carbohydrates, 0.76 g dietary fiber, 1.95 g fat, 21.4 mg cholesterol, 159 mg sodium, 62.0 mg potassium. Calories from protein: 11%; from carbohydrates: 73%; from fats: 16%.

CHOCOLATE CHIP BREAD

Chocolate and bread have a natural affinity. The flavors complement each other, providing a satisfying balance of sweetness and starch.

Depending on your model bread machine, either your loaf will come out with most of the chocolate chips whole, or, if your bread machine warms up during kneading and rising, the chocolate chips will melt to produce a rich chocolate dough. Whatever the outcome, the end result will be equally good.

2-CUP CAPACITY 12 SERVINGS	INGREDIENTS	3-CUP CAPACITY 16 SERVINGS
	YEAST	
1½ teaspoons	Active dry yeast	2¼ teaspoons
	DRY INGREDIENTS	
2 cups	Bread flour	3 cups
¾ teaspoon	Salt	1 teaspoon
1½ tablespoons	Granulated white sugar	2 tablespoons
1½ tablespoons	Dark brown sugar	2 tablespoons
2 tablespoons, plus 2 teaspoons	Nonfat dry milk	4 tablespoons
2 tablespoons	Unsalted butter or margarine	3 tablespoons
	LIQUID INGREDIENTS	
½ cup, plus 1 tablespoon	Water	1 cup
1 teaspoon	Vanilla extract	1½ teaspoons
1 large	Egg	1 large
1 teaspoon	Lemon juice	1 teaspoon
	CHOCOLATE CHIPS	
⅓ cup	Mini, semisweet chocolate chips	½ cup

All ingredients must be at room temperature, unless otherwise noted. Add ingredients in the order specified in your bread machine owner's manual. Add **chocolate chips** at the appropriate moment for your model bread machine. Set bread machine on the basic/standard bread making setting. If possible, select light baking cycle. If not, use medium or normal setting. Do not use the programmable timer when making this bread since the recipe contains perishable ingredients.

> **Nutrition information per ½-inch slice:**
> 139 calories, 3.33 g protein, 22.3 g carbohydrates, 0.81 g dietary fiber, 4.23 g fat, 23.1 mg cholesterol, 1.46 mg sodium, 72.7 mg potassium. Calories from protein: 10%; from carbohydrates: 63%; from fats: 27%.

BLACK CURRANT BREAD

Black currants are like small beads of honeylike sweetness. The dried fruit of the zante grape, currants are a favorite for baking.

2-CUP CAPACITY 12 SERVINGS	INGREDIENTS	3-CUP CAPACITY 16 SERVINGS
	YEAST	
1½ teaspoons	Active dry yeast	2¼ teaspoons
	DRY INGREDIENTS	
2 cups	Bread flour	3 cups
¾ teaspoon	Salt	1 teaspoon
1 teaspoon	Grated lemon zest	1½ teaspoons
4 teaspoons	Dark brown sugar	2 tablespoons
2 tablespoons, plus 1 teaspoon	Nonfat dry milk	4 tablespoons
2 teaspoons	Unsalted butter or margarine	1 tablespoon
	LIQUID INGREDIENTS	
½ cup	Water	1 cup
1 teaspoon	Vanilla extract	1½ teaspoons
1 large	Egg	1 large
1 teaspoon	Lemon juice	1 teaspoon
	BLACK CURRANTS	
⅓ cup	Dried black currants	½ cup

All ingredients must be at room temperature, unless otherwise noted. Add ingredients in the order specified in your bread machine owner's manual. Add **black currants** at the appropriate moment for your model bread machine. Set bread machine on the basic/standard bread making setting. If possible, select light baking cycle. If not, use medium or normal setting. Do not use the programmable timer when making this bread since the recipe contains perishable ingredients.

Nutrition information per ½-inch slice:
100 calories, 3.09 g protein, 20.4 g carbohydrates, 0.93 g dietary fiber, 1.91 g fat,
21.3 mg cholesterol, 144 mg sodium, 50.8 mg potassium. Calories from protein: 12%;
from carbohydrates: 70%; from fats: 18%.

SWISS CARAWAY BREAD

This quintessential sandwich bread is great with all kinds of cold cuts or toasted for breakfast. The addition of Swiss cheese adds a rich mellowness to this bread.

2-CUP CAPACITY 12 SERVINGS	INGREDIENTS	3-CUP CAPACITY 16 SERVINGS
	YEAST	
1½ teaspoons	Active dry yeast	2¼ teaspoons
	DRY INGREDIENTS	
2 cups	Bread flour	3 cups
½ cup	Shredded Swiss cheese	¾ cup
½ teaspoon	Caraway seeds	1 teaspoon
½ teaspoon	Dried mustard powder	¾ teaspoon
¾ teaspoon	Salt	1 teaspoon
2 teaspoons	Granulated white sugar	1 tablespoon
2 tablespoons	Nonfat dry milk	4 tablespoons
	LIQUID INGREDIENTS	
¾ cup	Water	1 cup, plus 2 tablespoons
1 teaspoon	Lemon juice	1 teaspoon

All ingredients must be at room temperature, unless otherwise noted. Add ingredients in the order specified in your bread machine owner's manual. Set bread machine on the basic/standard bread making setting. Select medium or normal baking cycle. Do not use the programmable timer when making this bread since the recipe contains perishable ingredients.

> **Nutrition information per ½-inch slice:**
> 100 calories, 3.87 g protein, 17.2 g carbohydrates, 0.68 g dietary fiber, 1.53 g fat, 4.45 mg cholesterol, 150 mg sodium, 47.2 mg potassium. Calories from protein: 16%; from carbohydrates: 70%; from fats: 14%.

SUN-DRIED TOMATO HERB BREAD

Originally prepared in the small villages of southern Italy to preserve the bulk of the tomato crop, sun-dried tomatoes were often used during the winter to make sauces and other dishes. When reconstituted in hot water, they have a very concentrated flavor and are also popular packed in extra-virgin olive oil and eaten as an appetizer or used as a garnish.

When sun-dried tomatoes are added to this bread dough, the result is a highly aromatic bread with the rich flavor of tomatoes and herbs.

2-CUP CAPACITY 12 SERVINGS	INGREDIENTS	3-CUP CAPACITY 16 SERVINGS
	YEAST	
1½ teaspoons	Active dry yeast	2¼ teaspoons
	DRY INGREDIENTS	
2 cups	Bread flour	3 cups
½ teaspoon	Dried oregano	¾ teaspoon
½ teaspoon	Dried basil	¾ teaspoon
1 teaspoon	Salt	1½ teaspoons
2 teaspoons	Granulated white sugar	1 tablespoon
	LIQUID INGREDIENTS	
¾ cup	Water	1 cup, plus 2 tablespoons
¼ cup	Coarsely chopped sun-dried tomatoes (see note)	⅓ cup
1 teaspoon	Lemon juice	1 teaspoon

All ingredients must be at room temperature, unless otherwise noted. Add ingredients in the order specified in your bread machine owner's manual. Set bread machine on the basic/standard bread making setting. Select medium or normal baking cycle. The programmable timer can be used, if desired.

NOTE: Sun-dried tomatoes are available in most supermarkets and specialty food stores. The best-tasting sun-dried tomatoes are packed in olive oil. Blot dry with paper towels to remove excess oil. Coarsely chop into small pieces.

Nutrition information per ½-inch slice:
77 calories, 2.28 g protein, 16.0 g carbohydrates, 0.68 g dietary fiber, 0.22 g fat, 179 mg cholesterol, 179 mg sodium, 31.9 mg potassium. Calories from protein: 12%; from carbohydrates: 85%; from fats: 3%.

RED PEPPER CUMIN BREAD

Red peppers add complexity to the flavor of a recipe and when they are combined with cumin seeds, the result is superb. When you use the whole seed and not powder, you are controlling the release of the aromatic flavor of the cumin to keep it from masking the flavor of the red peppers.

This bread is assertive enough to stand on its own, or it can be served with grilled meats or a Mexican-style stew or chili.

Allow at least one hour before making this bread for preparing the sautéed red peppers and letting them cool.

2-CUP CAPACITY 12 SERVINGS	INGREDIENTS	3-CUP CAPACITY 16 SERVINGS
	YEAST	
1½ teaspoons	Active dry yeast	2¼ teaspoons
	DRY INGREDIENTS	
2 cups	Bread flour	3 cups
½ teaspoon	Whole cumin seeds	¾ teaspoon
1 teaspoon	Salt	1½ teaspoons
2 teaspoons	Granulated white sugar	1 tablespoon
2 tablespoons	Nonfat dry milk	3 tablespoons
1 teaspoon	Unsalted butter or margarine	1½ teaspoons
	LIQUID INGREDIENTS	
½ cup, plus 1 tablespoon	Water	¾ cup, plus 3 tablespoons
¼ cup	Drained sautéed red pepper (see note)	⅓ cup
1 teaspoon	Lemon juice	1 teaspoon

All ingredients must be at room temperature, unless otherwise noted. Add ingredients in the order specified in your bread machine owner's manual. Set bread machine on the basic/standard bread making setting. Select medium or normal baking cycle. The programmable timer can be used, if desired.

NOTE: Cut 1 large red pepper in half. Remove seeds and coarsely chop. Coarsely chop 1 small white onion. Heat 2 tablespoons of olive oil in a small pan. Add onions and sauté approximately 5 minutes or until almost transparent (do not brown). Add chopped red pepper. Lower heat and sauté, approximately 10 minutes or until soft. Season to taste with salt and freshly ground black pepper. Remove from heat and let cool to room temperature.

Nutrition information per ½-inch slice:
85.8 calories, 2.55 g protein, 17.2 g carbohydrates, 0.71 g dietary fiber, 0.56 g fat, 0.99 mg cholesterol, 183 mg sodium, 47.1 mg potassium. Calories from protein: 12%; from carbohydrates: 82%; from fats: 6%.

ROASTED JALAPEÑO CHEESE BREAD

While far removed from authentic Mexican cuisine, roasted jalapeño cheese bread draws from a bounty of south-of-the-border ingredients that are readily available in most supermarkets. The roasted jalapeño peppers add an almost smoky flavor to the bread, while the coarsely ground cornmeal adds a nice crunch.

2-CUP CAPACITY 12 SERVINGS	INGREDIENTS	3-CUP CAPACITY 16 SERVINGS
	YEAST	
1½ teaspoons	Active dry yeast	2¼ teaspoons
	DRY INGREDIENTS	
2 cups	Bread flour	3 cups
½ cup	Shredded mild white Cheddar cheese	¾ cup
1½ teaspoons	Coarsely chopped roasted jalapeño peppers (see note)	2 teaspoons
1 tablespoon	Coarsely ground cornmeal	1½ tablespoons
¾ teaspoon	Salt	1 teaspoon
2 teaspoons	Granulated white sugar	1 tablespoon
2 tablespoons	Nonfat dry milk	4 tablespoons
	LIQUID INGREDIENTS	
¾ cup	Water	1 cup, plus 1 tablespoon

All ingredients must be at room temperature, unless otherwise noted. Add ingredients in the order specified in your bread machine owner's manual. Set bread machine on the basic/standard bread making setting. Select medium or normal baking cycle. Do not use the programmable timer when making this bread since the recipe contains perishable ingredients.

HINT: Baking with cheese in a bread machine can be tricky. Sometimes the enzymes in the cheese can work against the yeast and the bread can come out coarse with a flat or sunken top. Disappointed at first, I tried many different cheeses until I found that the milder ones like mild Cheddar and Swiss give the best results. I strongly recommend that you do not use any sharp or pungent cheeses.

NOTE: Roasted jalapeño peppers are available in jars or cans in most supermarkets and specialty food stores. Slice peppers in half. Cut off stems and remove seeds. Blot dry with paper towel.

Nutrition information per ½-inch slice:
104 calories, 3.74 g protein, 17.6 g carbohydrates, 0.72 g dietary fiber, 1.79 g fat, 5.08 mg cholesterol, 173 mg sodium, 106 mg potassium. Calories from protein: 15%; from carbohydrates: 69%; from fats: 16%.

PART TWO

HAND-SHAPED
DELIGHTS

BAGUETTES, BREAD STICKS, AND TWISTS

SWISS FARMHOUSE LOAVES

FLAT BREADS, PIZZAS, CALZONES, AND FOCACCIAS

BABKAS, BRAIDS, HOLIDAY BREADS, AND FRITTERS

BAGELS, BUNS, AND DANISH

BRIOCHE, PETITS PAINS, AND DOUGHNUTS

Cinnamon Coffee Bread (page 78)

Sun-Dried Tomato Herb Bread (page 88)

Greek Christopsomo Anise Bread (page 80)

Red Pepper Cumin Bread (page 90)

*Olive Oil Herb Grissini, Cheddar Cayenne Twists, and Sun-Dried
Tomato Herb Bread Sticks (pages 105, 106, and 107)*

Pain Paisan, Burebrot, and Partybrot (pages 114, 116, and 118)

Crisp Lavash and Soft Green-Onion Lavash (pages 126 and 128)

BAGUETTES, BREAD STICKS, AND TWISTS

The BREADS in this chapter are simple breads with unlimited appeal and versatility. Having virtually no fat and cholesterol, these breads are also good for you. Made from the simplest of ingredients: water, flour, yeast, perhaps some herbs and spices or a little cheese, these breads will entice even the most discriminating of palates.

I cannot think of anything more appealing than a crusty baguette with some well-ripened Brie and the perfect pear. Or, perhaps, a stew, rich with gravy, that demands to be sopped up with a piece of finely textured, crisp-crusted bread.

Bread sticks conjure up images of Italian restaurants where treasured family recipes are miraculously prepared in tiny kitchens. Perhaps the world's most perfect grazing food, with as little as 40 calories each, you can easily munch away on bread sticks without any guilt. Tied together in an attractive bundle, homemade bread sticks will make you a welcome guest wherever you bring them.

Pretzels made at home and eaten fresh from the oven take on a whole new appeal. With a thin, shiny crust and chewy texture, they hardly resemble the store-bought pretzels to which we are accustomed. Rather than just eating them as a snack food, do as the Swiss. Slice them in half to be used as a sandwich roll with some roasted ham and cheese, spread with mustard.

The Classic Margherita Pizza, Quattro Stagioni Pizza, and Eggplant Pizza (pages 138, 140, and 142)

BAGUETTES

Real French bread, or baguettes, as they are referred to in France, are thin, long, and crisp on the outside with a light crumb. Not at all like most of the rubbery batons sold in this country from coast to coast.

While we have always referred to this type of bread as "French" bread, it actually has its roots in many European countries—including Portugal, Spain, and Italy, where it is simply referred to as bread.

When baking baguettes, be sure to spray the oven walls with water a couple of times during the first 10 minutes of the baking process to produce the necessary steam to assure a crisp and shiny crust.

COUNTRY BAGUETTE

2-CUP CAPACITY 12 SERVINGS	INGREDIENTS	3-CUP CAPACITY 12 SERVINGS
	YEAST	
2¼ teaspoons	Active dry yeast	SAME AS FOR 2-CUP CAPACITY
	DRY INGREDIENTS	
3 cups	Bread flour	
2 tablespoons	Medium rye flour	
1½ teaspoons	Salt	
	LIQUID INGREDIENTS	
1¼ cups	Water	
1 teaspoon	Lemon juice	

MACHINE PROCEDURE: All ingredients must be at room temperature, unless otherwise noted. Add ingredients in the order specified in your bread machine owner's manual. Set bread machine on dough/manual setting. At the end of the program, press clear/stop. To punch dough down, press start and let knead for 60 seconds. Press clear/stop again. Remove dough and let rest 5 minutes before hand-shaping.

If your bread machine does not have a dough/manual setting, follow normal bread making procedure, but let dough knead only once. At the end of the kneading cycle, press clear/stop. Let dough rise for 60 minutes, checking after the first 30 minutes to make sure dough does not overrise and touch the lid. Press start and let machine run for 60 seconds to punch dough down. Press clear/stop. Remove dough and let rest 5 minutes before hand-shaping.

HAND-SHAPING TECHNIQUE: If using baking stones, place on the lowest rack of a cold oven. If using 13- x 9- x 1-inch baking pans, sprinkle lightly with fine cornmeal. Lightly sprinkle work surface with flour, place dough on floured area, and shape dough into a ball. If sticky, sprinkle lightly with flour. Cut into two equal pieces. Roll dough into a 10- x 6-inch rectangle with a lightly floured rolling pin. Fold rectangle of dough in half lengthwise. With the side of your hand, form a deep crease down the center of the dough. Fold dough over at crease. Securely pinch the seams together to form a tight cylinder. Roll the baguette over so that the seam is on the bottom. Quickly roll the baguette back and forth a few times working from the center out to the ends to stretch the baguette to the desired shape and length and to form pointed ends. Lightly sprinkle the work surface with flour as necessary so that the baguette does not stick. Place on baker's peel sprinkled lightly with fine cornmeal, or on prepared baking pan. With a very sharp paring knife or single-edge razor blade, cut top of loaf with ¼-inch-deep diagonal slashes at 2-inch intervals. Cover with a clean kitchen cloth. Let rise until doubled in size, about 1 to 1½ hours. Repeat procedure with remaining dough.

Preheat oven to 450° F. Bake for 25 to 30 minutes or until golden brown. Remove from oven and cool on wire rack.

Nutrition information per 1¼-inch slice:
119 calories, 3.49 g protein, 24.7 g carbohydrates, 1.15 g dietary fiber, 0.34 g fat, 0 mg cholesterol, 268 mg sodium, 47.2 mg potassium. Calories from protein: 12%; from carbohydrates: 85%; from fats: 3%.

WHEAT BAGUETTE

A fifty-fifty blend of white and whole-wheat flours gives this bread a richer crumb with more chew than a traditional baguette.

2-CUP CAPACITY	INGREDIENTS	3-CUP CAPACITY
12 SERVINGS		**12 SERVINGS**
	YEAST	
2¼ teaspoons	Active dry yeast	SAME AS FOR 2-CUP CAPACITY
	DRY INGREDIENTS	
1¾ cups	Bread flour	
1¾ cups	Whole-wheat flour	
1½ teaspoons	Salt	
1 teaspoon	Granulated white sugar	
	LIQUID INGREDIENTS	
1¼ cups, plus 1 tablespoon	Water	
1 teaspoon	Lemon juice	

Follow same machine procedure and hand-shaping technique as Country Baguette (see page 98).

Nutrition information per 1¼-inch slice:
193 calories, 6.66 g protein, 40.5 g carbohydrates, 4.26 g dietary fiber, 0.77 g fat, 0 mg cholesterol, 403 mg sodium, 151 mg potassium. Calories from protein: 14%; from carbohydrates: 83%; from fats: 4%.

SOURDOUGH BAGUETTE

Even if you have never been to San Francisco you have probably eaten sourdough bread in one form or another. Sourdough starter, the forerunner of today's yeast, was essential to making bread for thousands of years.

Today it is very easy to duplicate the wonderful taste and texture of breads made from a starter. By beginning this recipe the day before, you can easily make your own sourdough starter to be added to the bread recipe along with the other ingredients.

2-CUP CAPACITY	INGREDIENTS	3-CUP CAPACITY
12 SERVINGS		**12 SERVINGS**
	YEAST	
2 teaspoons	Active dry yeast	SAME AS FOR 2-CUP CAPACITY
	DRY INGREDIENTS	
3 cups	Bread flour	
1 teaspoon	Salt	
1½ tablespoons	Granulated white sugar	
¼ teaspoon	Baking soda	
	LIQUID INGREDIENTS	
¾ cup, plus 1 tablespoon	Water	
½ cup	Sourdough starter (see note)	

Follow same machine procedure and hand-shaping technique as Country Baguette (see page 98).

NOTE: Sourdough Starter

2¼ teaspoons	Active dry yeast
2 cups	Water
2 cups	Bread flour

To make sourdough starter, dissolve yeast in 2 cups of water in a clean gallon jar. Add flour and mix well. Starter mixture will thicken like batter. Cover jar opening with a clean cloth. Place in a warm location and let sit overnight or at least 12 hours before using.

(continued on the next page)

To replenish starter, always add flour and water equal to what was removed. For example, if you remove ½ cup of starter, add ½ cup of flour and ½ cup of water to the jar to replenish. Never add more than 1 cup of flour or water even if a greater amount of starter was used. Let starter stand at room temperature 12 hours before reusing. Store leftover starter in the refrigerator. Bring to room temperature before using again. It is normal that the starter may separate in the refrigerator and that the liquid may appear yellow in color. Stir well to blend before using. If starter discolors, develops mold, or is any color other than creamy white, discard and start over.

Nutrition information per 1¼-inch slice:
140 calories, 3.96 g protein, 29.4 g carbohydrates, 1.15 g dietary fiber, 0.37 g fat, 0 mg cholesterol, 197 mg sodium, 11.1 mg potassium. Calories from protein: 12%; from carbohydrates: 86%; from fats: 2%.

BREAD STICKS

Bread sticks, like potato chips, are addictive. Once you start eating them, it's hard to stop. At least most bread sticks are good for you. With very little or no fat at all, bread sticks come in a variety of shapes, flavors, and sizes.

The following recipes provide a sampling of how good bread sticks can be.

SESAME SEED BREAD STICKS

2-CUP CAPACITY ABOUT 18 BREAD STICKS	INGREDIENTS	3-CUP CAPACITY ABOUT 18 BREAD STICKS
	YEAST	
2¼ teaspoons	Active dry yeast	SAME AS FOR 2-CUP CAPACITY
	DRY INGREDIENTS	
3 cups	Bread flour	
1 teaspoon	Salt	
	LIQUID INGREDIENTS	
1 cup, plus 3 tablespoons	Water	
	TOPPINGS	
1 large	Egg white, beaten with 1 teaspoon water	
⅓ cup	Toasted sesame seeds	

MACHINE PROCEDURE: All ingredients must be at room temperature, unless otherwise noted. Add ingredients, except topping, in the order specified in your bread machine owner's manual. Set bread machine on dough/manual setting. At the end of the program, press clear/stop. To punch dough down, press start and let knead for 60 seconds. Press clear/stop again. Remove dough and let rest 5 minutes before hand-shaping.

If your bread machine does not have a dough/manual setting, follow normal bread making procedure, but let dough knead only once. At the end of the kneading cycle, press clear/stop. Let dough rise for 60 minutes, checking after the first 30 minutes to make sure dough does not overrise and touch the lid. Press start and let machine run for 60 seconds to punch dough down. Press clear/stop. Remove dough and let rest 5 minutes before hand-shaping.

(continued on the next page)

Hand-Shaping Technique: Prepare topping and set aside. Preheat oven to 375° F. Cut dough in half. On lightly floured work surface, roll out dough into a ¼-inch-thick rectangle. Cut lengthwise into ¼-inch-wide strips, 4 inches long. Carefully place on lightly greased baking pans. Brush with beaten egg white and sprinkle with sesame seeds. Bake approximately 20 minutes or until golden brown. Remove from oven and cool on wire rack.

Nutrition information per bread stick:
93.8 calories, 3.18 g protein, 16.2 g carbohydrates, 0.85 g dietary fiber, 1.72 g fat, 0 mg cholesterol, 124 mg sodium, 42.5 mg potassium. Calories from protein: 14%; from carbohydrates: 70%; from fats: 17%.

OLIVE OIL HERB GRISSINI

For best results, make these renowned bread sticks from Italy with a hand-cranked pasta maker if you have one. If not, roll dough with a rolling pin.

2-CUP CAPACITY ABOUT 36 BREAD STICKS	INGREDIENTS	3-CUP CAPACITY ABOUT 36 BREAD STICKS
	YEAST	
2¼ teaspoons	Active dry yeast	SAME AS FOR 2-CUP CAPACITY
	DRY INGREDIENTS	
3 cups	Bread flour	
1 teaspoon	Dried rosemary	
1 teaspoon	Coarsely ground black pepper	
1 teaspoon	Salt	
	LIQUID INGREDIENTS	
¾ cup, plus 3 tablespoons	Water	
¼ cup	Extra-virgin olive oil	

Follow same machine procedure as Sesame Seed Bread Sticks (see page 103).

HAND-SHAPING TECHNIQUE: Preheat oven to 375° F. Cut dough into four equal pieces. On lightly floured work surface, roll out dough into a ¼-inch-thick rectangle. Cut lengthwise into ¼-inch-wide strips, 12 inches long. Carefully place on lightly floured baking pans. Bake approximately 20 minutes or until golden brown. Let cool on wire rack.

If using a hand-cranked pasta maker, set the rollers on the widest opening. Flatten one piece of dough with the palm of your hand. Sprinkle with flour. Run the dough through the pasta maker. Sprinkle lightly with flour. Set the rollers two settings narrower (on the middle setting). Run the dough through again. Sprinkle lightly with flour and run the dough through the broad set of cutters used for cutting fettuccine or noodles. As the dough is cut, carefully gather on your fingers and remove. Lay flat on work surface and cut into lengths up to 14 inches long. Place on lightly floured baking pans. Bake approximately 10–15 minutes or until golden brown. Remove from oven and cool on wire rack.

Nutrition information per bread stick:
39.9 calories, 1.31 g protein, 7.98 g carbohydrates, 0.34 g dietary fiber, 0.20 g fat, 0 mg cholesterol, 59.7 mg sodium, 14.6 mg potassium. Calories from protein: 12%; from carbohydrates: 83%; from fats: 5%.

CHEDDAR CAYENNE TWISTS

With a flaky texture and the slight bite of cayenne pepper, these bread sticks are great with before-dinner drinks or with a steaming bowl of chili or soup. Make a double batch; they are guaranteed to vanish before you know it.

2-CUP CAPACITY	INGREDIENTS	3-CUP CAPACITY
ABOUT 24 BREAD STICKS		**ABOUT 24 BREAD STICKS**
	YEAST	
2¼ teaspoons	Active dry yeast	SAME AS FOR 2-CUP CAPACITY
	DRY INGREDIENTS	
3 cups	Bread flour	
¾ cup	Mild orange Cheddar cheese	
½ teaspoon	Ground cayenne pepper	
1 teaspoon	Ground mustard	
1 teaspoon	Salt	
	LIQUID INGREDIENTS	
1 cup, plus 2 tablespoons	Water	
	TOPPING	
2 teaspoons	Paprika	

Follow same machine procedure as Sesame Seed Bread Sticks (see page 103).

HAND-SHAPING TECHNIQUE: Preheat oven to 375° F. Cut dough in half. On lightly floured work surface, roll out dough with a floured rolling pin into a ¼-inch-thick rectangle. Cut lengthwise into ¼-inch-wide strips, 6 inches long. Carefully place on lightly greased baking pans. Gently twist. Sprinkle lightly with paprika. Bake approximately 20 minutes or until lightly golden. Remove from oven and cool on wire rack.

Nutrition information per bread stick:
72.4 calories, 2.61 g protein, 12.1 g carbohydrates, 0.55 g dietary fiber, 1.36 g fat, 3.72 mg cholesterol, 116 mg sodium, 30.9 mg potassium. Calories from protein: 15%; from carbohydrates: 68%; from fats: 17%.

SUN-DRIED TOMATO HERB BREAD STICKS

These crunchy bread sticks are reminiscent of the sun-ripened flavor of summer tomatoes. Great with Italian cheese, salami, and Chianti for a light al fresco supper.

2-CUP CAPACITY ABOUT 24 BREAD STICKS	INGREDIENTS	3-CUP CAPACITY ABOUT 24 BREAD STICKS
	YEAST	
2¼ teaspoons	Active dry yeast	SAME AS FOR 2-CUP CAPACITY
	DRY INGREDIENTS	
3 cups	Bread flour	
1 teaspoon	Salt	
1 teaspoon	Dried oregano	
	LIQUID INGREDIENTS	
1 cup, plus 2 tablespoons	Water	
¼ cup	Coarsely chopped sun-dried tomatoes (see note)	

Follow same machine procedure as Sesame Seed Bread Sticks (see page 103).

HAND-SHAPING TECHNIQUE: Preheat oven to 375° F. Cut dough in half. On lightly floured work surface, roll out dough with a floured rolling pin into a ¼-inch-thick rectangle. Cut lengthwise into ¼-inch-wide strips, 8 inches long. Carefully place on lightly greased baking pans. Bake approximately 20 minutes or until just beginning to brown. Remove from oven and cool on wire rack.

NOTE: Sun-dried tomatoes are available in most supermarkets and specialty food stores. The best tasting sun-dried tomatoes are packed in olive oil. Before chopping, blot with paper towels to remove excess oil.

Nutrition information per bread stick:
57.7 calories, 1.70 g protein, 12.0 g carbohydrates, 0.51 g dietary fiber, 0.164 g fat, 0 mg cholesterol, 89.6 mg sodium, 22.5 mg potassium. Calories from protein: 12%; from carbohydrates: 85%; from fats: 3%.

PRETZELS

Rumor has it that the first pretzels were made hundreds of years ago by a diligent, frugal monk who was also a baker. Tired of discarding his dough scraps, the monk decided to roll them out and knot them to resemble hands and arms in prayer.

Soft pretzels should be eaten within a few hours of being baked since they have a tendency to become soggy. You can, however, stick them in a 350° F. oven for approximately 10 minutes to recrisp.

BASIC PRETZEL

2-CUP CAPACITY	INGREDIENTS	3-CUP CAPACITY
ABOUT 8 PRETZELS		ABOUT 8 PRETZELS
	YEAST	
1½ teaspoons	Active dry yeast	SAME AS FOR 2-CUP CAPACITY
	DRY INGREDIENTS	
3 cups	Bread flour	
2 tablespoons	Light brown sugar	
	LIQUID INGREDIENTS	
1 cup, plus 3 tablespoons	Water	

FOR DUSTING/TOPPING
Coarse kosher or sea salt, for dusting baking pan and for sprinkling on pretzels (optional)

MACHINE PROCEDURE: All ingredients must be at room temperature, unless otherwise noted. Add ingredients, except for the salt, in the order specified in your bread machine owner's manual. Set bread machine on dough/manual setting. At the end of the first kneading cycle, press clear/stop. Remove dough and let rest 5 minutes before hand-shaping.

If your bread machine does not have a dough/manual setting, follow normal bread making procedure. At the end of the kneading cycle, press clear/stop. Remove dough and let rest 5 minutes before hand-shaping.

HAND-SHAPING TECHNIQUE: Fill a 3-quart saucepan with 2 quarts of water and ½ cup baking soda. Bring to a gentle boil.

Preheat oven to 475° F. Sprinkle two 13- x 9- x 1-inch baking pans with coarse salt. On lightly floured work surface, cut dough into eight equal pieces. Roll out each piece until it is a 16-inch-long rope. Make a U shape with each piece of dough. Cross the ends and twist. Pull the ends down and through the loops. Pinch to hold shape.

Place two pretzels at a time in the boiling water for approximately 15 seconds or until lightly golden in color. Remove and place four pretzels on each prepared baking pan. Sprinkle with additional salt, if desired. Bake for 8 to 10 minutes or until golden brown.

Nutrition information per pretzel (excluding surface salt):
198 calories, 5.0 g protein, 42.4 g carbohydrates, 1.41 g dietary fiber, 0.47 g fat, 0 mg cholesterol, 5.19 mg sodium, 83.4 mg potassium. Calories from protein: 10%; from carbohydrates: 88%; from fats: 2%.

OAT BRAN PRETZEL

Oat bran has been proven to help reduce cholesterol in some individuals by as much as 10 percent. Since pretzels have no cholesterol to begin with, I thought it would be great to add oat bran to create the ultimate, healthful snack food.

2-CUP CAPACITY	INGREDIENTS	3-CUP CAPACITY
ABOUT 8 PRETZELS		**ABOUT 8 PRETZELS**
	YEAST	
1½ teaspoons	Active dry yeast	SAME AS
		FOR 2-CUP
	DRY INGREDIENTS	CAPACITY
2½ cups	Bread flour	
½ cup	Oat bran	
2 tablespoons	Light brown sugar	
	LIQUID INGREDIENTS	
1 cup, plus	Water	
3 tablespoons		
	FOR DUSTING/TOPPING	
	Coarse kosher or sea salt, for dusting baking pan and for sprinkling on pretzels (optional)	

Follow same machine procedure and hand-shaping technique as Basic Pretzel (see page 108).

Nutrition information per pretzel (excluding surface salt):
177 calories, 5.22 g protein, 40.3 g carbohydrates, 2.23 g dietary fiber, 0.80 g fat, 0 mg cholesterol, 5.27 mg sodium, 108 mg potassium. Calories from protein: 11%; from carbohydrates: 85%; from fats: 4%.

WHEAT PRETZEL

Whole-wheat flour adds another twist to pretzels. In addition to the added fiber, the whole wheat adds texture and flavor.

2-CUP CAPACITY	INGREDIENTS	3-CUP CAPACITY
ABOUT 8 PRETZELS		**ABOUT 8 PRETZELS**
	YEAST	
1½ teaspoons	Active dry yeast	SAME AS FOR 2-CUP CAPACITY
	DRY INGREDIENTS	
1½ cups	Bread flour	
1½ cups	Whole-wheat flour	
2 tablespoons	Light brown sugar	
	LIQUID INGREDIENTS	
1 cup, plus 3 tablespoons	Water	
	FOR DUSTING/TOPPING	
	Coarse kosher or sea salt, for dusting baking pan and for sprinkling on pretzels (optional)	

Follow same machine procedure and hand-shaping technique as Basic Pretzel (see page 108).

Nutrition information per pretzel (excluding surface salt):
177 calories, 5.22 g protein, 40.3 g carbohydrates, 2.23 g dietary fiber, 0.80 g fat, 0 mg cholesterol, 5.27 mg sodium, 108 mg potassium. Calories from protein: 11%; from carbohydrates: 85%; from fats: 4%.

SWISS FARMHOUSE LOAVES

THE SWISS take bread seriously. Perhaps that can be attributed to the common belief that the first breads were made in what is today Switzerland, well over eight thousand years ago.

While very familiar with Swiss cheese, chocolates, and watches, on a recent visit to Switzerland, I was completely surprised by the variety and quality of their breads. Even in the smallest of villages, the local bread shops were well stocked with scores of loaves, from delicate breads made with butter and eggs, to the hearty, whole-grain loaves sprinkled with seeds and cracked grains. In some cases over twenty different varieties were available in a single tiny shop, each and every loaf a work of art.

After a few days in this beautiful country, I found it easy to understand why a Swiss meal is not complete without bread. Either robust in flavor and texture like the farmhouse loaf burebrot, or delicate and tender like the Bernese zopf, the wonderful recipes for handmade Swiss farmhouse loaves in this chapter demonstrate that the Swiss are indeed master bread bakers.

PAIN PAISAN

It never ceases to amaze me how we are content to pay up to four dollars for a loaf of coarse-textured country bread that cost only a fraction of that amount in Europe. Well, you need not spend your dollars on country breads anymore. Pain paisan is a Swiss recipe for a very basic, honest loaf of bread with a thick, crisp crust and chewy crumb. This very-easy-to-make bread is a hands-down winner.

2-CUP CAPACITY 2 LOAVES; 8 SERVINGS A LOAF	INGREDIENTS	3-CUP CAPACITY 2 LOAVES; 8 SERVINGS A LOAF
	YEAST	
1½ teaspoons	Active dry yeast	SAME AS FOR 2-CUP CAPACITY
	DRY INGREDIENTS	
2½ cups	Bread flour	
½ cup	Whole-wheat flour	
1½ teaspoons	Salt	
	LIQUID INGREDIENTS	
1¼ cups	Water	
1 teaspoon	Lemon juice	

MACHINE PROCEDURE: All ingredients must be at room temperature, unless otherwise noted. Add ingredients in the order specified in your bread machine owner's manual. Set bread machine on dough/manual setting. At the end of the program, press clear/stop. To punch dough down, press start and let knead for 60 seconds. Press clear/stop again. Remove dough and let rest 5 minutes before hand-shaping.

   If your bread machine does not have a dough/manual setting, follow normal bread making procedure but let dough knead only once. At the end of the kneading cycle, press clear/stop. Let dough rise for 60 minutes, checking after first 30 minutes to make sure dough does not overrise and touch the lid. Press start and let machine run for 60 seconds to punch down dough. Press clear/stop. Remove dough and let rest 5 minutes before hand-shaping.

HAND-SHAPING TECHNIQUE: If using baking stones, place on the lower rack of a cold oven. If using a 13- x 9- by 1-inch baking pan, dust with flour. Lightly sprinkle work surface with flour. Shape dough into a ball. If sticky, sprinkle lightly with flour. Cut in half. Using both hands, stretch ball of dough out and down. Gather the ends to the bottom center and pinch together to form a plump, round ball. Repeat this process a couple of times, or until the dough forms into a smooth, tight loaf. Gently pinch together bottom ends. You should now have a perfectly round, smooth ball of dough.

Carefully place the loaf on a well-floured baker's peel or the prepared baking pan. With a very sharp paring knife or single-edge razor blade, cut the top of the loaf with a large X, approximately ¼-inch deep. Cover with a clean kitchen cloth. Let rise until doubled in size, about 1 to 1½ hours. Repeat the same procedure with the remaining dough.

Preheat oven to 425° F. When loaf has doubled in size, sprinkle it generously with flour and place in preheated oven. Bake for approximately 30 minutes or until brown in color. Remove from oven and cool on wire rack.

Nutrition information per ½-inch slice:
84.5 calories, 2.62 g protein, 17.7 g carbohydrates, 1.08 g dietary fiber, 0.27 g fat, 0 mg cholesterol, 201 mg sodium, 41.3 mg potassium. Calories from protein: 13%; from carbohydrates: 85%; from fats: 3%.

BUREBROT

Breads baked and purchased at supermarket bakeries are more often than not limp and tasteless. The only exceptions I have ever encountered are the wonderful breads Swiss hausfraus buy every day at their local Migros supermarkets.

The breads on display would be the envy of any baker. Both the hearty loaves and the finer, buttery creations are the works of true artisans.

One of my favorite loaves bought at the Migros in Basel was Burebrot, a true farmhouse loaf like the loaves someone's grandmother used to make from the farm's own grains. Darker in color than pain paisan, this bread goes well with everything.

2-CUP CAPACITY	INGREDIENTS	3-CUP CAPACITY
16 SERVINGS		16 SERVINGS
	YEAST	
1½ teaspoons	Active dry yeast	SAME AS FOR 2-CUP CAPACITY
	DRY INGREDIENTS	
1½ cups	Bread flour	
¾ cup	Whole-wheat flour	
¾ cup	Medium rye flour	
1½ teaspoons	Salt	
	LIQUID INGREDIENTS	
1¼ cups	Water	
1 teaspoon	Lemon juice	

MACHINE PROCEDURE: All ingredients must be at room temperature, unless otherwise noted. Add ingredients in the order specified in your bread machine owner's manual. Set bread machine on dough/manual setting. At the end of the program, press clear/ stop. To punch dough down, press start and let knead for 60 seconds. Press clear/stop again. Remove dough and let rest 5 minutes before hand-shaping.

If your bread machine does not have a dough/manual setting, follow normal bread making procedure but let dough knead only once. At the end of the kneading cycle, press clear/stop. Let dough rise for 60 minutes, checking after first 30 minutes to make sure dough does not overrise and touch the lid. Press start and let machine run for 60 seconds to punch down dough. Press clear/stop. Remove dough and let rest 5 minutes before hand-shaping.

Hand-Shaping Technique: If using baking stones, place on the lower rack of a cold oven. If using a 13- x 9- by 1-inch baking pan, dust with flour. Lightly sprinkle work surface with flour. Shape dough into a ball. Lightly sprinkle with flour. With lightly floured rolling pin, roll out to 14- x 6-inch rectangle. Fold ends into center. Fold sides into center. Pinch center seam together. Turn loaf over. Pinch each end to form a point and tuck under loaf. With floured hands, gently mold into an oval.

Carefully place the loaf on a well-floured baker's peel or the prepared baking pan. With a very sharp paring knife or single-edge razor blade, cut the top of the loaf with ¼-inch diagonal slashes at 1-inch intervals. Cover with a clean kitchen cloth. Let rise until doubled in size, about 1 to 1½ hours.

Preheat oven to 425° F. When loaf has doubled in size, sprinkle generously with flour and place in preheated oven. Bake for approximately 30 minutes or until brown in color. Remove from oven and cool on wire rack.

Nutrition information per ½-inch slice:
80 calories, 2.51 g protein, 16.8 g carbohydrates, 1.80 g dietary fiber, 0.31 g fat, 0 mg cholesterol, 201 mg sodium, 56.8 mg potassium. Calories from protein: 13%; from carbohydrates: 84%; from fats: 3%.

PARTYBROT

One of the most interesting-looking breads we kept coming across during our travels in Switzerland were these large, round loaves of bread that appeared to be many small rolls attached together. Little did we know that we were looking at partybrot, a specialty of Swiss-German bakers.

Partybrot is indeed made up of rolls from different types of doughs that are hand-shaped and placed together in a round baking pan. Sprinkled with different kinds of seeds, served at parties and get-togethers, the baked result is both attractive and festive.

**2 LOAVES;
13 SERVINGS EACH**

INGREDIENTS

1 recipe	Pain paisan (see page 114)
1 recipe	Burebrot (see page 116) (see note)

TOPPING

3 tablespoons	Sesame seeds, poppy seeds, millet seeds, rolled oats, or cracked wheat

HAND-SHAPING TECHNIQUE: Lightly sprinkle work surface with flour. Shape pain paisan dough into a ball and, with floured hands, roll dough on work surface to form a 19-inch-long cylinder. Repeat same procedure with burebrot dough. Cut each cylinder into 13 equal pieces. Shape each piece into a perfect ball of dough by stretching out and down a couple of times, always pinching together the bottom edges.

In a lightly greased 9-inch round baking pan, place one ball of dough in the center. Place six balls of dough around the center ball, alternating the type of dough. Space evenly (they will touch and connect as they rise). Cover with a clean kitchen cloth and let rise until doubled, about 1 to 1½ hours. Repeat the same procedure with the remaining dough.

Preheat the oven to 425° F. When doubled in size, brush the partybrot with water. Sprinkle the individual rolls with seeds or grains. For a greater effect, sprinkle the center roll with one kind of seed and the outer rolls with two other kinds of seeds and grains, alternating the flavors. Bake in preheated oven on center rack for approximately 30 to 35 minutes or until golden brown. Remove from oven. Let cool for 10 minutes. Carefully remove bread from pan and cool on wire rack.

NOTE: While the second dough is being made, take first and place in a lightly greased, large mixing bowl. Cover with a clean kitchen cloth and place in the refrigerator to slow down the rising process. Remove from refrigerator 20 minutes before the second dough is ready.

Nutrition information per single roll without topping:
101 calories, 3.16 g protein, 21.2 g carbohydrates, 1.77 g dietary fiber, 0.36 g fat, 0 mg cholesterol, 247.5 mg sodium, 60.5 mg potassium. Calories from protein: 13%; from carbohydrates: 84%; from fats: 3%.

ZOPF

On Saturday mornings the street-corner bread vendors in Switzerland proudly display their golden-brown loaves of zopf. A rich milk-and-egg braid that stays fresh and soft for a couple of days, zopf is eaten by the Swiss on Sundays, when the bakers take a much deserved day off.

This wonderful bread is easy to make and turns a beautiful golden brown when baked.

2-CUP CAPACITY 12 SERVINGS	INGREDIENTS	3-CUP CAPACITY 12 SERVINGS
	YEAST	
2¼ teaspoons	Active dry yeast	SAME AS FOR 2-CUP CAPACITY
	DRY INGREDIENTS	
3 cups	Bread flour	
1 teaspoon	Salt	
½ teaspoon	Granulated white sugar	
4 tablespoons	Unsalted butter or margarine	
	LIQUID INGREDIENTS	
¾ cup	Water	
1 large	Egg	
1 large	Egg yolk	
	EGG WASH	
1 large	Egg, beaten with 2 pinches salt	

MACHINE PROCEDURE: All ingredients must be at room temperature, unless otherwise noted. Add ingredients, except egg wash, in the order specified in your bread machine owner's manual. Set bread machine on dough/manual setting. At the end of the program, press clear/stop. To punch dough down, press start and let knead for 60 seconds. Press clear/stop again. Remove dough and let rest 5 minutes before hand-shaping.

If your bread machine does not have a dough/manual setting, follow normal bread making procedure but let dough knead only once. At the end of the kneading cycle, press clear/stop. Let dough rise for 60 minutes, checking after first 30 minutes to make sure dough does not overrise and touch the lid. Press start and let machine run for 60 seconds to punch down dough. Press clear/stop. Remove dough and let rest 5 minutes before hand-shaping.

HAND-SHAPING TECHNIQUE: Lightly sprinkle work surface with flour. Divide dough into three equal pieces. Dampen hands and roll each piece into a 16-inch-long rope. Sprinkle dough with flour if too sticky. Lay ropes next to each other and pinch top ends together. Braid the ropes and pinch the remaining ends together. Place on a lightly greased 13- x 9- x 1-inch baking pan. Tuck ends under. Cover with a clean kitchen cloth and let rise until doubled in size, about 1 to 1½ hours, and set aside.

Preheat oven to 375° F. Prepare egg wash. Brush braid with egg wash. Wait 5 minutes. Brush again. Wait 15 minutes to let egg wash dry. Bake for 30 minutes or until golden brown. Remove from oven and cool on wire rack.

Nutrition information per 1-inch slice:
102 calories, 3.50 g protein, 18.6 g carbohydrates, 0.76 g dietary fiber, 1.25 g fat, 28.2 mg cholesterol, 144 mg sodium, 55.1 mg potassium. Calories from protein: 14%; from carbohydrates: 75%; from fats: 11%.

GUGELHOPF

The first time I ever had a gugelhopf was in Switzerland. It was my friend Dieter's birthday and his wife Jacqueline had made one for him. In Dieter's family, along with the customary birthday cake, his grandmother, Lena, would make the birthday celebrant a gugelhopf. Traditionally made in a high, ridged, crownlike pan, gugelhopf is a rich and buttery yeast bread filled with currants and almonds and sprinkled with confectioners' sugar.

2-CUP CAPACITY	INGREDIENTS	3-CUP CAPACITY
16 SERVINGS		**16 SERVINGS**
	YEAST	
2¼ teaspoons	Fast-rise yeast	SAME AS FOR 2-CUP CAPACITY
	DRY INGREDIENTS	
3¼ cups	All-purpose unbleached flour	
½ teaspoon	Salt	
½ cup	Granulated white sugar	
½ teaspoon	Grated lemon zest	
	LIQUID INGREDIENTS	
1 cup	Milk	
1 large	Egg	
4 tablespoons	Melted unsalted butter or margarine	
	FRUIT AND NUTS	
½ cup	Dried black currants	
¼ cup	Slivered almonds	
	FOR DUSTING	
	Confectioners' sugar	

MACHINE PROCEDURE: All ingredients must be at room temperature, unless otherwise noted. Add ingredients, except for **fruit and nuts** and confectioners' sugar, in the order specified in your bread machine owner's manual. Set bread machine on dough/manual setting. Add **fruit and nuts** 10 minutes after first kneading cycle begins. Press clear/stop at the end of the first kneading cycle. Let the dough rise for 1 hour, or until doubled in size, checking after the first 30 minutes to make sure dough does not overrise and touch the lid. Press start and let machine run for 60 seconds to punch dough down. Press clear/stop again. Remove dough and let rest 5 minutes before hand-shaping.

If your bread machine does not have a dough/manual setting, follow normal bread making procedure. Add **fruit and nuts** 10 minutes after the first kneading cycle begins. At the end of the first kneading cycle, press clear/stop. Let dough rise for 60 minutes or until almost doubled in size, checking after first 30 minutes to make sure dough does not overrise and touch the lid. Press start and let machine run for 60 seconds to punch down the dough. Press clear/stop. Let rest 5 minutes before removing.

HAND-SHAPING TECHNIQUE: Generously butter gugelhopf pan. If one is not available, use an angel food pan. Flour your hands. Remove dough from bread machine. Dough will be sticky. With your fingers, make a hole in the center of the dough as if you were forming a large doughnut. Put dough in the pan, letting pan tube come through hole in center of dough. Gently pat dough to spread evenly. Cover with a clean kitchen cloth and let rise 1 to 1½ hours, or until dough is almost to top of pan. Preheat oven to 350° F. Bake for approximately 50 minutes. The gugelhopf is done when a toothpick inserted in the center comes out clean. Remove gugelhopf from pan and cool on wire rack. Sprinkle generously with confectioners' sugar before serving.

Nutrition information per ½-inch slice:
185 calories, 4.27 g protein, 30.9 g carbohydrates, 1.33 g dietary fiber, 5.07 g fat, 23.1 mg cholesterol, 79.8 mg sodium, 118 mg potassium. Calories from protein: 9%; from carbohydrates: 66%; from fats: 24%.

FLAT BREADS, PIZZAS, CALZONES, AND FOCACCIAS

Most people think that pizza, calzone, and focaccia are purely Italian in origin, but they are actually the result of the Islamic influence in Italy from the eighth to the fifteenth centuries. Many of the inhabitants of the Islamic Empire, which stretched from Morocco to China, were prolific traders who, in addition to exchanging silks and spices, helped introduce many different foods to the Mediterranean cuisine through trade. While Northern Europe was in the midst of the Dark Ages, the Arabic dynasties of the Mediterranean basin and the Middle East were flourishing and enjoying a cultural and culinary renaissance. This Arabic influence on the cuisine of the empire's diverse territories can be seen today in the similarity between the soft lavash breads of the Middle East and the chewy focaccias of southern Italy.

In addition, there are as many varieties of flat breads as there were Arabic dynasties and tribes. Flat breads are usually relatively thin, with just enough leavening agent for the finished bread to be soft and pliable. For this reason, they are ideally suited to be wrapped, stuffed, or spread with different toppings or used in place of an eating utensil to scoop up tasty concoctions of regional specialties. Or you can make flat breads as crisp as crackers by leaving out the fats or oils from the basic recipe. These diverse breads, whether served plain, stuffed, or covered with a spread, are always most enjoyable when eaten without knife and fork and simply picked up in your hands.

CRISP LAVASH

Crisp lavash is like eating a cracker, only better. With no added fat or cholesterol, this Armenian flat bread can be enjoyed by everyone. By adding different toppings, you can make either plain, sweet, or savory lavashes.

The trick to making the lavash crisp is to roll out the dough as thin as possible. If you happen to have a hand-cranked pasta maker you're in luck. If you are rolling the dough by hand, be patient and roll the dough as thin as possible. It will be well worth your effort.

2-CUP CAPACITY 24 SERVINGS	INGREDIENTS	3-CUP CAPACITY 24 SERVINGS
	YEAST	
1½ teaspoons	Active dry yeast	SAME AS FOR 2-CUP CAPACITY
	DRY INGREDIENTS	
1 cup	Bread flour	
1 cup	Whole-wheat flour	
1 teaspoon	Salt	
2 tablespoons	Nonfat dry milk	
	LIQUID INGREDIENTS	
¾ cup, plus 2 tablespoons	Water	
	MILK WASH	
2 tablespoons	Milk	
	TOPPING	
2 tablespoons	Lightly toasted sesame seeds, poppy seeds, millet seeds, or cracked wheat	

MACHINE PROCEDURE: All ingredients must be at room temperature, unless otherwise noted. Add ingredients, except for **milk wash and topping**, in the order specified in your bread machine owner's manual. Set bread machine on dough/manual setting. At the end of the program, press clear/stop. To punch the dough down, press start and let knead for 60 seconds. Press clear/stop again. Remove dough and let rest 5 minutes before hand-shaping.

If your bread machine does not have a dough/manual setting, follow normal bread making procedure but let dough knead only once. At the end of the kneading cycle, press clear/stop. Let dough rise for 60 minutes, checking after first 30 minutes to make sure dough does not overrise and touch the lid. Press start and let machine run for 60 seconds to punch the dough down. Press clear/stop. Remove dough and let rest 5 minutes before hand-shaping.

HAND-SHAPING TECHNIQUE: Preheat oven to 400° F. Cut dough into four equal pieces. On a lightly floured work surface, roll out the dough as thin as possible. Square off the edges. Cut into 4- x 3-inch rectangles. Place on lightly floured 13- x 9- x 1-inch baking pans. Lightly brush with milk wash and sprinkle with toasted seeds. Bake for 10 minutes or until the lavash are beginning to brown.

If you are using a hand-cranked pasta maker, set the rollers on the widest opening. Flatten one piece of dough with the palm of your hand. Sprinkle with flour. Run the dough through the pasta maker. Sprinkle lightly with flour. Set the rollers two settings narrower (on the middle setting). Run the dough through again. Sprinkle lightly with flour. Set the rollers on the narrowest setting. Run the dough through one last time. Place on lightly floured work surface. Square off the edges. Cut into 4- x 3-inch rectangles. Place on lightly floured baking pans. Lightly brush with milk wash and sprinkle with toasted seeds. Bake for 10 minutes or until the lavash are just beginning to brown.

Nutrition information per 4- x 3-inch lavash without toppings:
37.6 calories, 1.40 g protein, 7.79 g carbohydrates, 0.82 g dietary fiber, 0.15 g fat, 0.06 mg cholesterol, 91.5 mg sodium, 35.1 mg potassium. Calories from protein: 15%; from carbohydrates: 82%; from fats: 4%.

LAVASH VARIATIONS

Lavash are extremely versatile and can be eaten any time of the day as a low-calorie snack. The following toppings can be sprinkled on the lavash, in lieu of the seeds, before baking.

CINNAMON AND SUGAR LAVASH

24 SERVINGS

2 tablespoons	Granulated white sugar
1 teaspoon	Ground cinnamon

Mix well. Sprinkle on prepared lavash in place of seeds. Bake as directed.

GARLIC AND ONION LAVASH

24 SERVINGS

1 teaspoon	Garlic powder
1 teaspoon	Onion powder

Mix well. Sprinkle on prepared lavash in place of seeds. Bake as directed.

SOFT GREEN-ONION LAVASH

Soft lavash is like a big sheet of chewy pita bread, only better since it is also made with sweet green onions. Since soft lavash dries out very quickly, always store it in a sealed plastic bag to assure freshness.

2-CUP CAPACITY	INGREDIENTS	3-CUP CAPACITY
8 SERVINGS		8 SERVINGS
	YEAST	
2 teaspoons	Active dry yeast	SAME AS
		FOR 2-CUP
	DRY INGREDIENTS	CAPACITY
3 cups	Bread flour	
¼ cup	Finely sliced scallion tops	
1½ teaspoons	Salt	
1 tablespoon	Granulated white sugar	
2 tablespoons	Vegetable shortening	
	LIQUID INGREDIENTS	
1 cup, plus	Water	
3 tablespoons		

MACHINE PROCEDURE: All ingredients must be at room temperature, unless otherwise noted. Add ingredients in the order specified in your bread machine owner's manual. Set bread machine on dough/manual setting. At the end of the program, press clear/stop. To punch the dough down, press start and let knead for 60 seconds. Press clear/stop again. Remove dough and let rest 5 minutes before hand-shaping.

If your bread machine does not have a dough/manual setting, follow normal bread making procedure but let dough knead only once. At the end of the kneading cycle, press clear/stop. Let dough rise for 60 minutes, checking after first 30 minutes to make sure dough does not overrise and touch the lid. Press start and let machine run for 60 seconds to punch the dough down. Press clear/stop. Remove dough and let rest 5 minutes before hand-shaping.

HAND-SHAPING TECHNIQUE: Position oven rack on lowest position. Preheat oven and 13- x 9- x 1-inch baking pan to 425° F., 30 minutes before you plan to bake the lavash.

Cut dough into two equal pieces. On a lightly floured work surface, roll out dough into two ¼-inch-thick, free-form ovals. Place on preheated baking pan sprinkled lightly with flour. Bake for approximately 10 to 12 minutes or until lavash puffs up and is a light golden brown. Lavash should be soft. Do not overbake or lavash will become crisp. Place hot baked lavash in a large, clean, brown paper bag. Fold over top to seal. As lavash cools it will remain soft.

Nutrition information for ¼ sheet of lavash:
208 calories, 5.11 g protein, 37.5 g carbohydrates, 1.54 g dietary fiber, 3.69 g fat, 0 mg cholesterol, 402 mg sodium, 71.1 mg potassium. Calories from protein: 10%; from carbohydrates: 74%; from fats: 16%.

PITA BREAD

Up until a few years ago pita bread was sold only in Arabic and Greek neighborhoods. Today it is as popular and well known as good ole American white bread.

When cut in half, pita breads form a pocket which can be stuffed with meat, cheese, or vegetables. They can also be split in half and cut into triangles. Bake these triangles at 375° F. for approximately 5 minutes or until crisp, and use in place of high-calorie chips or crackers.

BASIC PITA BREAD

2-CUP CAPACITY	INGREDIENTS	3-CUP CAPACITY
12 SERVINGS		12 SERVINGS
	YEAST	
2¼ teaspoons	Active dry yeast	SAME AS FOR 2-CUP CAPACITY
	DRY INGREDIENTS	
3 cups	Bread flour	
1½ teaspoons	Salt	
¾ teaspoon	Granulated white sugar	
1 tablespoon	Vegetable shortening	
	LIQUID INGREDIENTS	
1 cup, plus 3 tablespoons	Water	

MACHINE PROCEDURE: All ingredients must be at room temperature, unless otherwise noted. Add ingredients in the order specified in your bread machine owner's manual. Set bread machine on dough/manual setting. At the end of the program, press clear/stop. To punch the dough down, press start and let knead for 60 seconds. Press clear/stop again. Remove dough and let rest 5 minutes before hand-shaping.

If your bread machine does not have a dough/manual setting, follow normal bread making procedure but let dough knead only once. At the end of the kneading cycle, press clear/stop. Let dough rise for 60 minutes, checking after first 30 minutes to make sure dough does not overrise and touch the lid. Press start and let machine run for 60 seconds to punch the dough down. Press clear/stop. Remove dough and let rest 5 minutes before hand-shaping.

HAND-SHAPING TECHNIQUE: Place 13- x 9- x 1-inch baking pan in oven. Preheat oven to 500° F. On lightly floured work surface, cut dough in half and cut each half into six equal pieces. Lightly sprinkle with flour. Shape pieces into smooth balls. With a lightly floured rolling pin, roll each ball into a flat 4-inch disk. Lightly sprinkle both sides with flour. Cover with a clean kitchen cloth and let rise 30 minutes on work surface. Place four pita breads on preheated baking pan. Bake approximately 5 minutes or until breads puff up and just begin to brown. Remove from oven and cool on wire rack. Continue baking remaining pita breads, four at a time. Breads will collapse as they cool. If they don't, prick them with a fork.

Nutrition information per plain pita bread:
125 calories, 3.39 g protein, 24.1 g carbohydrates, 0.99 g dietary fiber, 1.38 g fat, 0 mg cholesterol, 268 mg sodium, 43 mg potassium. Calories from protein: 11%; from carbohydrates: 79%; from fats: 10%.

WHEAT PITA BREAD

The addition of whole-wheat flour adds fiber and flavor to this pita bread variation.

2-CUP CAPACITY 12 SERVINGS	INGREDIENTS	3-CUP CAPACITY 12 SERVINGS
	YEAST	
2¼ teaspoons	Active dry yeast	SAME AS FOR 2-CUP CAPACITY
	DRY INGREDIENTS	
1½ cups	Bread flour	
1½ cups	Whole-wheat flour	
1½ teaspoons	Salt	
¾ teaspoon	Granulated white sugar	
1 tablespoon	Vegetable shortening	
	LIQUID INGREDIENTS	
1¼ cups	Water	

Follow same machine procedure and hand-shaping technique as for Basic Pita Bread (see page 130).

Nutrition information per Wheat Pita Bread:
119 calories, 3.83 g protein, 23.1 g carbohydrates, 2.46 g dietary fiber, 1.51 g fat, 0 mg cholesterol, 268 mg sodium, 87 mg potassium. Calories from protein: 13%; from carbohydrates: 76%; from fats: 11%.

PITA BREAD VARIATIONS

You can add any combination of herbs and spices to the Basic Pita Bread or Wheat Pita Bread recipe. Two particular favorites follow.

ONION AND GARLIC PITA BREAD

Add ½ teaspoon each onion and garlic powder to dry ingredients when preparing the dough. Use as bread or serve as chips with a garbanzo bean spread as an appetizer.

TEX-MEX PITA BREAD

Add ½ teaspoon each chili powder and paprika to dry ingredients when preparing the dough. Split them in half to make tacos or serve them as chips with guacamole.

INDIAN NAAN

Naan, a white flour flat bread from India, is traditionally made in a brick and clay tandoor oven. This flat bread can also be easily made in a conventional oven by baking the rounds of dough on a baking stone or tiles or on a preheated baking pan placed directly on the bottom of a hot oven.

Naan does not brown like other breads. It should be baked only for 60 seconds or less. It will still be white although with perhaps a couple of brown spots like a cooked flour tortilla. Wrap seasoned grilled meats, seafood, or vegetables with pieces of naan. Naan should be served immediately after preparing.

2-CUP CAPACITY 8 SERVINGS	INGREDIENTS	3-CUP CAPACITY 8 SERVINGS
	YEAST	
1½ teaspoons	Active dry yeast	SAME AS FOR 2-CUP CAPACITY
	DRY INGREDIENTS	
2 cups	Bread flour	
1 teaspoon	Salt	
	LIQUID INGREDIENTS	
½ cup, plus 1 tablespoon	Water	
2 tablespoons	Clarified butter (see note)	

MACHINE PROCEDURE: All ingredients must be at room temperature, unless otherwise noted. Add ingredients in the order specified in your bread machine owner's manual. Set bread machine on dough/manual setting. At the end of the first kneading, press clear/stop. Remove dough and let rest 5 minutes before hand-shaping.

If your bread machine does not have a dough/manual setting, follow normal bread making procedure, but let dough knead only once. At the end of the kneading cycle, press clear/stop. Remove dough and let rest 5 minutes before hand-shaping.

HAND-SHAPING TECHNIQUE: Place 13- x 9- x 1-inch baking pan on bottom of oven. Preheat oven to 500° F. On lightly floured work surface, cut dough in half and cut into four equal pieces. With a lightly floured rolling pin, roll each piece into a ¼-inch-thick free-form circle. Cover with a clean kitchen cloth and let rest 20 minutes. Lightly sprinkle tops with flour and roll out as thin as possible. Place 1 to 2 naans face down on preheated baking pan. Bake 60 seconds. Remove from oven. Place on large plate and cover with a clean kitchen cloth. Continue baking remaining naans. Eat warm.

NOTE: To make clarified butter, melt 4 tablespoons of unsalted butter over low heat. Skim off and discard any foam that may have accumulated and reserve the remaining clear, golden liquid. This is the clarified butter, or ghee as it is known in Indian cooking. Discard any solids left in saucepan.

Nutrition information per piece of naan:
140 calories, 3.42 g protein, 23.9 g carbohydrates, 0.99 g dietary fiber, 3.19 g fat, 7.77 mg cholesterol, 292 mg sodium, 43.8 mg potassium. Calories from protein: 10%; from carbohydrates: 69%; from fats: 21%.

PIZZA

As far as fast food goes, pizza is probably the most nutritious, especially when made at home using healthy ingredients like low-fat cheese, fresh vegetables, and whole-wheat flour for the crust.

Pizza is a versatile food that allows for much creativity—by experimenting with doughs and toppings, you can make an endless variety of pizzas.

BASIC PIZZA DOUGH

2-CUP CAPACITY 8 SLICES	INGREDIENTS	3-CUP CAPACITY 8 SLICES
	YEAST	
1½ teaspoons	Active dry yeast	SAME AS FOR 2-CUP CAPACITY
	DRY INGREDIENTS	
3 cups	Bread flour	
1 teaspoon	Salt	
	LIQUID INGREDIENTS	
1¼ cups	Water	

WHOLE-WHEAT PIZZA DOUGH

2-CUP CAPACITY	INGREDIENTS	3-CUP CAPACITY
	YEAST	
1½ teaspoons	Active dry yeast	SAME AS FOR 2-CUP CAPACITY
	DRY INGREDIENTS	
2½ cups	Bread flour	
½ cup	Whole-wheat flour	
1 teaspoon	Salt	
	LIQUID INGREDIENTS	
1¼ cups	Water	

MACHINE PROCEDURE: Choose either Basic Pizza Dough or Whole-Wheat Pizza Dough recipe. All ingredients must be at room temperature, unless otherwise noted. Add ingredients in the order specified in your bread machine owner's manual. Set bread machine on dough/manual setting. At the end of the first kneading cycle, press clear/stop. Let dough rise for 60 minutes. Check after 30 minutes to make sure dough does not overrise and touch lid. To punch down dough, press start and let knead for 60 seconds. Press clear/stop again. Remove dough and let rest 5 minutes before hand-shaping.

If your bread machine does not have a dough/manual setting, follow normal bread making procedure, but let dough knead only once. At the end of the kneading cycle, press clear/stop. Let dough rise for 60 minutes. Check after 30 minutes to make sure dough does not overrise and touch lid. Press start and let machine run for 60 seconds to punch down dough. Press clear/stop again. Remove dough and let rest 5 minutes before hand-shaping.

THE CLASSIC MARGHERITA PIZZA

If you ever go to Italy and decide to order pizza, you'll find the experience somewhat overwhelming. Here we either order a regular or Sicilian pie and then choose from a variety of toppings. In Italy, each pizza has its own identity and name to go with it. The Margherita is basically what we know to be a plain pizza; however, in keeping with the true tradition of Neapolitan cooking, this wonderful pizza also has the addition of fresh basil as one of its toppings.

This is truly a classic among pizzas.

8 SLICES

INGREDIENTS
1 recipe Basic Pizza Dough or Whole-Wheat Pizza Dough (see page 136).

MARGHERITA PIZZA TOPPINGS

TOMATO SAUCE

1 28-ounce can	Plum tomatoes, crushed, with their liquid
3 tablespoons	Extra-virgin olive oil
	Salt and freshly ground black pepper to taste

BASIL AND CHEESES

16 leaves	Fresh basil, washed and dried
8 ounces	Shredded mozzarella cheese
2 tablespoons	Grated Parmesan cheese

Combine the tomatoes and the olive oil in a medium-size saucepan. Bring to a boil. Lower heat to a simmer. Cover and cook for 5 minutes. Remove cover and let simmer. Cover and cook for 5 minutes. Remove cover and let simmer an additional 5 minutes. Season to taste with salt and pepper. (Refrigerate or freeze any leftover sauce.) Set aside the sauce, basil and cheeses to top the pizza. Yields approximately 2 cups of sauce.

MACHINE PROCEDURE: Prepare one recipe Basic Pizza Dough or Whole-Wheat Pizza Dough (see page 136).

HAND-SHAPING TECHNIQUE: If you plan to bake your pizza directly on a baking stone or tiles, place on the lower rack of cold oven. Preheat oven to 450° F. at least 30 minutes before you plan to bake pizza. Lightly sprinkle a baker's peel with finely ground cornmeal. Cut ball of dough in four equal pieces. Sprinkle lightly with flour. On baker's peel, roll out a piece of dough with a floured rolling pin into a ¼-inch-thick free-form oval or circle. Spread top of pizza with sauce, in a thin layer. Lay four fresh basil leaves on top. Sprinkle with one-quarter of the shredded mozzarella and one-quarter of the Parmesan. Slide pizza onto preheated baking stone. Repeat procedure with remaining dough and topping. Bake for approximately 20 minutes or until topping is bubbly and crust is lightly golden.

Carefully remove baked pizza from oven with baker's peel or spatula. Cut each pizza in half to make two slices.

If using a pizza pan or baking sheet, lightly grease with olive or vegetable oil. Preheat oven to 425° F. Lightly sprinkle ball of dough with flour. With fingertips and the heel of your hand, spread dough evenly into a 16-inch round pizza pan or 13- x 9- x 1-inch baking pan. If dough does not stretch easily, let rest for 5 minutes and continue. Spread top of pizza with a thin layer of sauce. Lay fresh basil leaves on top. Sprinkle with shredded mozzarella cheese and grated Parmesan. Bake for approximately 20 minutes, or until topping is bubbly and crust is lightly golden.

Remove from oven. Slice pizza into eight equal pieces.

Nutrition information per slice made with Basic Pizza Dough:
347 calories, 12.9 g protein, 40.6 g carbohydrates, 2.52 g dietary fiber, 14.6 g fat,
27.9 mg cholesterol, 631 mg sodium, 331 mg potassium. Calories from protein: 15%;
from carbohydrates: 47%; from fats: 38%.

Nutrition information per slice made with Whole-Wheat Pizza Dough:
344 calories, 13.1 g protein, 40.1 g carbohydrates, 3.25 g dietary fiber, 14.6 g fat,
27.9 mg cholesterol, 631 mg sodium, 353 mg potassium. Calories from protein:
15%; from carbohydrates: 47%; from fats: 38%.

QUATTRO STAGIONI

Quattro Stagioni, which means "four seasons," is a pizza divided into four parts. Each part, through its toppings, represents a different season of the year.

The following toppings are to be used only as a guide. Be creative and make your own favorite combinations. Just remember: spring should always have something green; summer, tomatoes and basil; fall, mushrooms; and winter, only a combination of white cheeses and cured ham.

8 SLICES

INGREDIENTS
1 recipe Basic Pizza Dough or Whole-Wheat Pizza Dough (see page 136).

QUATTRO STAGIONI TOPPINGS

SPRING

¾ cup	Steamed, chopped broccoli
1 cup	Ricotta cheese
2 tablespoons	Grated Parmesan cheese

SUMMER

⅓ cup	Tomato Sauce (See Margherita Pizza Topping, page 138)
½ cup	Shredded mozzarella cheese
2 teaspoons	Grated Parmesan cheese
4 leaves	Fresh basil, washed and dried

FALL

⅓ cup	Tomato Sauce (see Margherita Pizza Topping, page 138)
½ cup	Sliced fresh mushrooms
2 cloves	Garlic, finely minced
2 teaspoons	Coarsely chopped parsley
2 tablespoons	Grated Parmesan cheese

WINTER

½ cup	Shredded mozzarella cheese
¼ cup	Shredded fontina cheese
¼ cup	Shredded provolone cheese
¼ cup	Finely minced prosciutto or smoked ham

MACHINE PROCEDURE: Prepare one recipe Basic Pizza Dough or Whole-Wheat Pizza Dough (see page 136).

HAND-SHAPING TECHNIQUE: Lightly grease a 13- x 9- x 1-inch baking pan with olive or vegetable oil. Preheat oven to 425° F. Lightly sprinkle ball of dough with flour. With fingertips and the heel of your hand, spread dough evenly into the baking pan. If dough does not stretch easily, let rest for 5 minutes and continue. Visually divide pizza into four equal sections. Layer ingredients on appropriate sections. Bake for approximately 20 minutes or until topping is bubbly and crust is lightly golden. Remove from oven. Slice pizza into eight equal pieces.

Approximate nutrition information per slice made with Basic Pizza Dough:
320 calories, 9.29 g protein, 41.4 g carbohydrates, 2.69 g dietary fiber, 11.8 g fat, 20 mg cholesterol, 627 mg sodium, 369.3 mg potassium. Calories from protein: 14%; from carbohydrates: 55%; from fats: 31%.

Approximate nutrition information per slice made with Whole-Wheat Pizza Dough:
318 calories, 12.43 g protein, 40.9 g carbohydrates, 3.43 g dietary fiber, 11.82 g fat, 20 mg cholesterol, 627 mg sodium, 391 mg potassium. Calories from protein: 14%; from carbohydrates: 55%; from fats: 31%.

EGGPLANT PIZZA

This recipe combines pizza with an old-time favorite: eggplant parmigiana.

8 SLICES

INGREDIENTS

1 recipe Basic Pizza Dough or Whole-Wheat Pizza Dough (see page 136).

EGGPLANT TOPPING

¼ cup	Extra-virgin olive oil
1 medium	Eggplant, peeled and sliced thin
1 cup	Tomato Sauce (see Margherita Pizza Topping recipe, page 138)
8 ounces	Shredded mozzarella cheese
¼ cup	Grated Parmesan cheese

Heat olive oil in large skillet over medium heat. Sauté eggplant slices 2 to 3 minutes on each side until golden. Drain on paper towels to absorb excess oil. Set aside eggplant, sauce, mozzarella, and Parmesan to top pizza.

MACHINE PROCEDURE: Prepare one recipe Basic Pizza Dough or Whole-Wheat Pizza Dough (see page 136).

HAND-SHAPING TECHNIQUE: If you plan to bake your pizza directly on baking stone or tiles, place on the lower rack of cold oven. Preheat oven to 450° F. at least 30 minutes before you plan to bake pizza. Lightly sprinkle a baker's peel with finely ground cornmeal. Cut ball of dough in four equal pieces. Sprinkle lightly with flour. On baker's peel, roll out a piece of dough with a floured rolling pin into a ¼-inch-thick free-form oval or circle. Cover pizza with mozzarella cheese. Layer eggplant slices on top in spiral fashion, overlapping slightly. Cover with tomato sauce. Sprinkle with grated Parmesan cheese.

Slide pizza onto preheated baking stone. Repeat procedure with remaining dough. Bake for approximately 20 minutes or until topping is bubbly and crust is lightly golden.

Carefully remove baked pizza from oven with baker's peel or spatula. Cut each pizza in half to make two slices.

If using a pizza pan or baking sheet, lightly grease with olive or vegetable oil. Preheat oven to 425° F. Lightly sprinkle ball of dough with flour. With fingertips and the heel of your hand, spread dough evenly into a 16-inch round pizza pan or 13- x 9- x 1-inch baking pan. If dough does not stretch easily, let rest for 5 minutes and continue. Spread top of pizza with prepared topping as directed above. Bake for approximately 20 minutes or until topping is bubbly and crust is lightly golden. Remove from oven. Slice pizza into eight equal pieces.

Nutrition information per slice made with Basic Pizza Dough:
374 calories, 13.2 g protein, 40.4 g carbohydrates, 2.93 g dietary fiber, 17.6 g fat, 28.9 mg cholesterol, 680 mg sodium, 285 mg potassium. Calories from protein: 14%; from carbohydrates: 43%; from fats: 43%.

Nutrition information per slice made with Whole-Wheat Pizza Dough:
371 calories, 13.4 g protein, 39.9 g carbohydrates, 3.67 g dietary fiber, 17.7 g fat, 28.9 mg cholesterol, 680 mg sodium, 307 mg potassium. Calories from protein: 14%; from carbohydrates: 43%; from fats: 43%.

PIZZA FRITTA

Small fried dough pockets filled with creamy ricotta cheese have long been a favorite snack food in southern Italy. Pizza fritta, which literally means "fried pie," is a delicious counterpart to our street-corner hot dog.

INGREDIENTS
1 recipe Basic Pizza Dough (see page 136).

PIZZA FRITTA FILLING
15 ounces   Ricotta cheese, part-skim or whole-milk

FOR FRYING
Vegetable oil

12 SERVINGS

MACHINE PROCEDURE: Prepare one recipe Basic Pizza Dough (see page 136).

HAND-SHAPING TECHNIQUE: On lightly floured work surface, roll dough into a 12-inch-long cylinder. Cut dough into twelve equal pieces. Lightly sprinkle balls of dough with flour. Roll out each ball of dough into a 1/8-inch-thick circle. Place 1 well-rounded tablespoon of ricotta cheese in the center of each circle. With your fingertip, wet the inside edge of the circle with water. Fold the dough over to make a half-moon and seal. Fold the edges up and crimp so that the pizza is well sealed.

In a heavy, deep skillet, heat 1 inch of vegetable oil to 375° F. Gently place two pizza frittas in the oil at a time. After approximately 2 minutes turn over and continue frying for another 1 to 2 minutes or until golden brown on both sides. Drain well on paper towel. Eat warm.

Nutrition information per Pizza Fritta:
273 calories, 11.9 g protein, 24.3 g carbohydrates, 0.94 g dietary fiber, 13.8 g fat, 35.9 mg cholesterol, 416 mg sodium, 90.5 mg potassium. Calories from protein: 18%; from carbohydrates: 36%; from fats: 46%.

CALZONES

A calzone is a stuffed pie that resembles a very large turnover. In fact, the name *calzone* reportedly comes from the Italian word for trousers, since it looks like an overstuffed pants leg. Although not exactly low in calories (perhaps that's the connection with a "stuffed" pair of pants), a calzone, along with a green salad, is a meal in itself.

2-CUP CAPACITY 6 Servings	INGREDIENTS	3-CUP CAPACITY 6 Servings
	YEAST	
1½ teaspoons	Active dry yeast	SAME AS FOR 2-CUP CAPACITY
	DRY INGREDIENTS	
3 cups	Bread flour	
1 teaspoon	Salt	
½ teaspoon	Granulated white sugar	
	LIQUID INGREDIENTS	
1 cup, plus 2 tablespoons	Water	
2 tablespoons	Olive oil	
	CHEESE FILLING	
15 ounces	Ricotta cheese, part skim or whole milk	
½ cup	Shredded mozzarella cheese	
¼ cup	Grated Parmesan cheese	

Mix the three cheeses together.

	SAUSAGE FILLING	
3	Sweet Italian sausages	
1 tablespoon	Vegetable oil	

In heavy skillet cook sausages in 1 tablespoon oil. Cool to room temperature and slice into ¼-inch pieces.

MACHINE PROCEDURE: All ingredients must be at room temperature, unless otherwise noted. Add ingredients in the order specified in your bread machine owner's manual.

(continued on the next page)

Set bread machine on dough/manual setting. At the end of the first kneading cycle, press clear/stop. Let dough rise until doubled in size, about 1 to 1½ hours. Check every 30 minutes to make sure dough does not overrise and touch lid. To punch dough down, press start and let knead for 60 seconds. Press clear/stop again. Remove dough and let rest 5 minutes before hand-shaping.

If your bread machine does not have a dough/manual setting, follow normal bread making procedure, but let dough knead only once. At the end of the kneading cycle, press clear/stop. Let dough rise until doubled in size, about 1 to 1½ hours. Check every 30 minutes to make sure dough does not overrise and touch lid. Press start and let machine run for 60 seconds to punch dough down. Press clear/stop again. Remove dough and let rest 5 minutes before hand-shaping.

HAND-SHAPING TECHNIQUE: Prepare fillings and set aside. Preheat oven to 400° F. On lightly floured work surface, roll dough into 6-inch-long cylinder. Cut dough into six equal pieces. Lightly sprinkle balls of dough with flour. Roll out each ball of dough into a ¼-inch-thick circle. Place one sixth of the cheese filling in the center of each circle. Place one sixth of the sausage slices on top of the cheese. With your fingertip, wet the inside edge of the circle with water. Fold the dough over to make a half-moon and seal. Fold the edge up and crimp so that the calzone is well sealed. Place on lightly oiled baking sheets. Bake for 25 minutes or until golden brown. Serve hot.

Nutrition information per Calzone:
601 calories, 28.2 g protein, 52.2 g carbohydrates, 1.88 g dietary fiber, 30.2 g fat, 74.6 mg cholesterol, 985 mg sodium, 300 mg potassium. Calories from protein: 19%; from carbohydrates: 35%; from fats: 46%.

PIZZA ROLL-UPS

Like a baked sandwich, Pizza Roll-Ups are sheets of bread dough covered with a savory filling, rolled up and baked. When sliced, you have a delicious, spiral sandwich. Be creative and invent your own fillings.

BASIC PIZZA ROLL-UP DOUGH

2-CUP CAPACITY 12 SLICES	INGREDIENTS	3-CUP CAPACITY 12 SLICES
	YEAST	
1½ teaspoons	Active dry yeast	SAME AS FOR 2-CUP CAPACITY
	DRY INGREDIENTS	
3 cups	Bread flour	
1½ teaspoons	Salt	
½ teaspoon	Granulated white sugar	
	LIQUID INGREDIENTS	
¾ cup, plus 2 tablespoons	Water	
3 tablespoons	Extra-virgin olive oil	
2 tablespoons	Milk	
	EGG WASH	
1 large	Egg, beaten with 1 tablespoon water	

MACHINE PROCEDURE: All ingredients must be at room temperature, unless otherwise noted. Add ingredients, except for egg wash, in the order specified in your bread machine owner's manual. Set bread machine on dough/manual setting. At the end of the program, press clear/stop. To punch dough down, press start and let knead for 60 seconds. Press clear/stop again. Remove dough and let rest 5 minutes before hand-shaping.

If your bread machine does not have a dough/manual setting, follow normal bread making procedure, but let dough knead only once. At the end of the kneading cycle, press clear/stop. Let dough rise for 60 minutes, checking after the first 30 minutes to make sure dough does not overrise and touch lid. Press start and let machine run for 60 seconds to punch down dough. Press clear/stop. Remove dough and let rest 5 minutes before hand-shaping.

(continued on the next page)

HAND-SHAPING TECHNIQUE: Prepare filling of your choice (suggested ones follow). Preheat oven to 400° F. Lightly grease 13- x 9- x 1-inch baking pan with vegetable oil or parchment paper. Generously sprinkle work surface with flour. Roll out dough into 16- x 12-inch rectangle. Make sure dough does not stick to work surface.

PIZZA ROLL-UP FILLINGS

PEPPERS AND EGG PIZZA ROLL-UP

1 pound	Sweet frying peppers
2 tablespoons	Extra-virgin olive oil
4 cloves	Garlic, finely minced
	Salt and fresh ground black pepper to taste
3 large	Eggs
¼ cup	Grated Parmesan cheese

Wash and dry peppers. Cut in half. Remove stems and seeds. Cut lengthwise into thin strips. Heat oil in large skillet. Add garlic and peppers. Sauté over medium heat until soft. Season with salt and pepper. Beat eggs with ¼ cup Parmesan cheese and add this mixture to the skillet. Remove immediately from burner. Mix well to coat peppers with eggs. Eggs will solidify only slightly. Let cool to room temperature. Spread over prepared dough. Roll up as tightly as possible in jelly-roll fashion so that you will have a 16-inch-long roll when completed. Pinch long seam closed as well as ends. Tuck ends under. Carefully place on prepared baking pan, seam side down. Brush top with egg wash. Prick six times with a fork along the top and sides. Bake for 30 to 35 minutes, or until golden brown. Let cool on wire rack 20 minutes before slicing.

Nutrition information per 1¼-inch slice:
210 calories, 6.85 g protein, 26.4 g carbohydrates, 1.46 g dietary fiber, 8.41 g fat, 73 mg cholesterol, 242 mg sodium, 104 mg potassium. Calories from protein: 13%; from carbohydrates: 51%; from fats: 36%.

BROCCOLI AND CHEESE PIZZA ROLL-UP

1 pound	Chopped broccoli, steamed
½ cup	Shredded mozzarella cheese
½ pound	Sliced provolone cheese
2 cloves	Garlic, finely minced
1 tablespoon	Grated Parmesan cheese
2 tablespoons	Lightly toasted sesame seeds

Cool steamed broccoli to room temperature. Layer sliced provolone over prepared dough and cover evenly with prepared broccoli. Sprinkle with garlic and cheeses. Roll up as tightly as possible in jelly-roll fashion so that you will have a 16-inch-long roll when completed. Pinch long seam closed as well as ends. Tuck ends under. Carefully place on prepared baking pan, seam side down. Brush top with egg wash and sprinkle with sesame seeds. Prick six times with a fork along the top and sides. Bake for 30 to 35 minutes, or until golden brown. Let cool on wire rack 20 minutes before slicing.

Nutrition information per 1¼-inch slice:
294 calories, 13.6 g protein, 27.1 g carbohydrates, 2.3 g dietary fiber, 14.5 g fat, 45.2 mg cholesterol, 485 mg sodium, 225 mg potassium. Calories from protein: 19%; from carbohydrates: 37%; from fats: 45%.

SALAMI AND CHEESE PIZZA ROLL-UP

¼ pound	Sliced provolone cheese
¼ pound	Genoa salami
½ cup	Shredded mozzarella cheese
1 tablespoon	Grated Parmesan cheese
1 tablespoon	Poppy seeds

Layer sliced provolone cheese and salami over prepared dough. Sprinkle with shredded mozzarella cheese and grated Parmesan cheese. Roll up as tightly as possible in jelly-roll fashion so that you will have a 16-inch-long roll when completed. Pinch long seam closed as well as ends. Tuck ends under. Carefully place on prepared baking pan, seam side down. Brush top with egg wash and sprinkle with poppy seeds. Prick six times with a fork along the top and sides. Bake for 30 to 35 minutes, or until golden brown. Let cool on wire rack 20 minutes before slicing.

Nutrition information per 1¼-inch slice:
264 calories, 11.1 g protein, 24.8 g carbohydrates, 0.94 g dietary fiber, 12.9 g fat, 44.3 mg cholesterol, 474 mg sodium, 102 mg potassium. Calories from protein: 17%; from carbohydrates: 38%; from fats: 45%.

FOCACCIA

Nana's "pizza" was always chewy and thick, covered with fresh, garlicky tomato sauce with plenty of basil and sprinkled with sharp Pecorino Romano cheese. Little did we know what we were eating was focaccia.

Focaccia embodies all the flavors and scents of the Mediterranean kitchen. A coarse, chewy slab of baked bread dough covered with olive oil, coarse salt, and whatever herbs and vegetables there may be on hand, focaccia can be as simple or as flavorful as you want it to be. The toppings that can be used on focaccia are endless. Be creative, keeping in mind focaccia's Mediterranean origins for the most authentic results.

BASIC FOCACCIA

2-CUP CAPACITY	INGREDIENTS	3-CUP CAPACITY
12 SERVINGS		**12 SERVINGS**
	YEAST	
2¼ teaspoons	Active dry yeast	SAME AS FOR 2-CUP CAPACITY
	DRY INGREDIENTS	
3 cups	Bread flour	
½ teaspoon	Salt	
½ teaspoon	Sugar	
	LIQUID INGREDIENTS	
1 cup, plus 2 tablespoons	Water	
1 tablespoon	Olive oil	
	BASIC FOCACCIA TOPPING	
2 tablespoons	Extra-virgin olive oil	
2 teaspoons	Coarse salt (kosher or sea salt)	
	Fresh ground black pepper to taste	

MACHINE PROCEDURE: All ingredients must be at room temperature, unless otherwise noted. Add ingredients, except toppings, in the order specified in your bread machine owner's manual. Set bread machine on dough/manual setting. At the end of the program, press clear/stop. To punch dough down, press start and let knead for 60 seconds. Press clear/stop again. Remove dough and let rest 5 minutes before hand-shaping.

If your bread machine does not have a dough/manual setting, follow normal bread making procedure, but let dough knead only once. At the end of the kneading cycle, press clear/stop. Let dough rise for 60 minutes, checking after the first 30 minutes to make sure dough does not overrise and touch lid. Press start and let machine run for 60 seconds to punch dough down. Press clear/stop again. Remove dough and let rest 5 minutes before hand-shaping.

HAND-SHAPING TECHNIQUE: Sprinkle hands with flour. With fingertips, spread dough evenly into a 13- x 9- x 1-inch lightly oiled baking pan. Cover with a clean kitchen cloth. Let rise until doubled in height, about 30 to 60 minutes.

Preheat oven to 400° F. Make light indentations with your fingertips in the surface of the risen dough. Brush with extra-virgin olive oil and sprinkle with coarse salt and black pepper. Bake on bottom rack of oven for approximately 30 to 35 minutes, or until golden brown. Let cool in pan. Cut into twelve equal pieces and serve at room temperature.

Nutrition information per slice of Basic Focaccia:
218 calories, 5.12 g protein, 36.1 g carbohydrates, 1.51 g dietary fiber, 5.54 g fat, 0 mg cholesterol, 669 mg sodium, 66.1 mg potassium. Calories from protein: 10%; from carbohydrates: 67%; from fats: 23%.

FRESH HERB FOCACCIA

A perfect way to take advantage of a bumper crop of summer herbs.

12 Servings

INGREDIENTS
1 recipe Basic Focaccia Dough, prepared up to the baking stage (see page 150)

HERB TOPPING

¼ cup   Coarsely chopped fresh herbs (rosemary, basil, sage, oregano, thyme, etc., or any combination of herbs with complementary flavors)

Sprinkle unbaked focaccia with the chopped herbs. Bake on bottom rack of the preheated 400° F. oven for approximately 30 to 35 minutes, or until golden brown. Let cool in pan. Cut into twelve equal pieces and serve at room temperature.

Nutrition information per slice of Herb Focaccia:
218 calories, 5.12 g protein, 36.1 g carbohydrates, 1.51 g dietary fiber, 5.54 g fat, 0 mg cholesterol, 669 mg sodium, 66.1 mg potassium. Calories from protein: 10%; from carbohydrates: 67%; from fats: 23%.

ONION AND SAGE FOCACCIA

The sweet caramelized flavor of onions and the fragrance of sage make this focaccia a personal favorite.

12 SERVINGS

INGREDIENTS
1 recipe Basic Focaccia Dough prepared up to the baking stage (see page 150)

ONION AND SAGE TOPPING

2 large	Yellow onions, peeled and sliced thin
6 tablespoons	Extra-virgin olive oil
¼ cup	Fresh sage leaves
1½ teaspoons	Coarse salt (either kosher or sea salt)
	Freshly ground black pepper to taste

Sauté sliced onions in 4 tablespoons of oil over low heat in a medium-size pan until onions are soft and transparent. Do not brown. Spread sautéed onions over unbaked focaccia. Cover with fresh sage leaves. Sprinkle with salt and season with pepper to taste. Drizzle with remaining 2 tablespoons of oil. Bake on bottom rack of preheated 400° F. oven for approximately 30 to 35 minutes, or until golden brown. Let cool in pan. Cut into twelve equal pieces and serve at room temperature.

Nutrition information per slice of Onion and Sage Focaccia:
283 calories, 5.24 g protein, 37.2 g carbohydrates, 1.71 g dietary fiber, 12.3 g fat, 0 mg cholesterol, 670 mg sodium, 82.9 mg potassium. Calories from protein: 7%; from carbohydrates: 54%; from fats: 39%.

PLUM TOMATO AND PECORINO ROMANO FOCACCIA

A close rendition of Nana's "pizza."

12 SERVINGS

INGREDIENTS

1 recipe Basic Focaccia Dough prepared up to the baking stage (see page 150)

TOMATO AND PECORINO ROMANO TOPPING

4 cloves	Garlic, peeled and crushed
2 tablespoons	Extra-virgin olive oil
1 28-ounce can	Plum tomatoes, crushed, with their liquid
¼ cup	Whole fresh basil leaves
3 tablespoons	Minced Italian parsley
	Salt and fresh ground·black pepper to taste
3 tablespoons	Grated Pecorino Romano cheese

Prepare sauce by sautéing garlic in oil over low heat in a medium-size pan. Add tomatoes, salt, pepper, basil, and parsley. Simmer for 30 minutes, or until sauce is thick, stirring occasionally. Spread a thin layer of tomato sauce over the unbaked focaccia. Sprinkle with the grated cheese and bake on the bottom rack of the preheated 400° F. oven for approximately 30 to 35 minutes, or until bubbly. Let cool in pan. Cut into twelve equal pieces and serve at room temperature.

Nutrition information per slice of Tomato and Pecorino Romano Focaccia:
280 calories, 6.95 g protein, 41.3 g carbohydrates, 2.75 g dietary fiber, 9.78 g fat, 2.21 mg cholesterol, 857 mg sodium, 320 mg potassium. Calories from protein: 10%; from carbohydrates: 59%; from fats: 31%.

BABKAS, BRAIDS, HOLIDAY BREADS, AND FRITTERS

Loaves of rich yeast dough filled with dried fruits, chocolate, cheese, or cured meats can tempt even the most disciplined of dieters. Usually prepared for special occasions or holidays, the breads in this chapter shout celebration. With the assistance of your bread machine, you can easily prepare these breads for your family and friends any day of the year.

In the past, rich yeast breads were prepared only a couple of times a year because ingredients such as butter, eggs, and white flour were too costly for ordinary people to buy on a daily basis. Careful planning and hoarding of ingredients were essential to making these breads. Although we do not have to concern ourselves with such issues today, these breads still play an important role in our celebrations and connect us to our ancestors and our heritage. Since we are truly one large culinary melting pot, many of these breads have crossed over cultural boundaries and have been adopted and adapted by us with great ease.

Years ago, when many homes did not have ovens, doughs and batters would be prepared at home and then taken to the neighborhood bakery for baking when the ovens were not in use and while they were still hot. This required careful planning on the part of the home baker and is probably one explanation for why every culture has at least one favorite fried yeast confection that could be made at home whenever desired. Made from very simple ingredients, fried doughnuts and fritters hold a special place in most cultures' bread repertoires.

BABKA

Babka is a sweet bread made from rich yeast dough that is filled with chocolate, cheese, or buttery crumbs. Originally from Eastern Europe, babka makes a wonderful breakfast bread or is perfect later in the day with a cup of coffee.

The following is a recipe for basic cinnamon sugar babka. Suggested recipes for chocolate and cheese babka fillings also follow. Prepare the crumb topping and the desired filling while the dough is rising.

2-CUP CAPACITY 12 SERVINGS	INGREDIENTS	3-CUP CAPACITY 12 SERVINGS
	YEAST	SAME AS FOR 2-CUP CAPACITY
2½ teaspoons	Active dry yeast	
	DRY INGREDIENTS	
3½ cups	Unbleached all-purpose flour	
½ teaspoon	Salt	
2 tablespoons	Granulated white sugar	
2 tablespoons	Unsalted butter or margarine	
	LIQUID INGREDIENTS	
1 cup, plus 2 tablespoons	Milk	
2 large	Eggs	
½ teaspoon	Vanilla extract	
	CINNAMON SUGAR BABKA FILLING	
2 tablespoons	Unsalted butter, softened	
¼ cup	Granulated white sugar	
1 teaspoon	Ground cinnamon	
	CRUMB TOPPING	
1 tablespoon	Unsalted butter, softened	
2 tablespoons	Granulated white sugar	
2 tablespoons	Unbleached all-purpose flour	
2 pinches	Ground cinnamon	
	EGG WASH	
1 large	Egg white, beaten with 1 teaspoon water	

Machine Procedure: All ingredients must be at room temperature, unless otherwise noted. Add ingredients, except for filling, crumb topping, and egg wash, in the order specified in your bread machine owner's manual. Set bread machine on dough/manual setting. At the end of the program, press clear/stop. To punch dough down, press start and let knead for 60 seconds. Press clear/stop again. Remove dough and let rest 5 minutes before hand-shaping.

If your bread machine does not have a dough/manual setting, follow normal bread making procedure but let dough knead only once. At the end of the kneading cycle, press clear/stop. Let dough rise for 60 minutes, checking after the first 30 minutes to make sure dough does not overrise and touch the lid. Press start and let machine run for 60 seconds to punch dough down. Press clear/stop. Remove dough and let rest 5 minutes before hand-shaping.

Hand-Shaping Technique: While the dough is rising, prepare your filling of choice by blending ingredients together with a fork until crumbly. To make crumb topping, blend all ingredients together with a fork until crumbly. Chill both until ready to use. Lightly grease a 4½- x 8½-inch loaf pan. On a lightly floured work surface, roll the dough into a 10- x 20-inch rectangle. Cover with filling up to 1 inch from the edges. Roll up lengthwise, jelly-roll fashion. Pinch seam and ends securely together so that they do not open during baking. Carefully place babka in prepared pan. Fold ends under and shape into an S so that it fits in pan. Cover with a clean kitchen cloth and let rise until doubled in size.

Preheat oven to 350° F. Form a crease in the top of the risen babka with the side of your hand. Brush with egg wash and cover with crumb topping. Bake approximately 30 to 35 minutes, or until golden brown. If babka begins to brown too quickly, cover top with foil. Remove from pan and cool on a wire rack.

Nutrition information per ¾-inch slice of Cinnamon Sugar Babka:
231 calories, 5.66 g protein, 38.1 g carbohydrates, 1.20 g dietary fiber, 6.02 g fat, 48.7 mg cholesterol, 109 mg sodium, 86.6 mg potassium. Calories from protein: 10%; from carbohydrates: 66%; from fats: 24%.

VARIATIONS

CHOCOLATE BABKA FILLING

¼ cup	Unsweetened cocoa
½ cup	Granulated white sugar
¼ cup	Melted, unsalted butter
⅓ cup	Coarsely chopped pecans

(continued on the next page)

Blend together unsweetened cocoa and sugar. Brush surface of babka with melted butter. Sprinkle with cocoa-sugar mixture and pecans.

Nutrition information per ¾-inch slice of Chocolate Babka:
274 calories, 6.26 g protein, 39.5 g carbohydrates, 1.94 g dietary fiber, 10.5 g fat, 53.9 mg cholesterol, 110 mg sodium, 121 mg potassium. Calories from protein: 9%; from carbohydrates: 57%; from fats: 34%.

CHEESE BABKA FILLING

8 ounces	Farmer cheese
2 tablespoons	Granulated white sugar
1 tablespoon	Unbleached, all-purpose flour
1 large	Egg yolk
2 teaspoons	Grated orange zest
¼ cup	Dark raisins

Blend together all the ingredients but the raisins. After spreading the cheese filling on the babka, sprinkle with raisins.

Nutrition information per ¾-inch slice of Cheese Babka:
232 calories, 8.28 g protein, 38.8 g carbohydrates, 1.48 g dietary fiber, 4.62 g fat, 62.1 mg cholesterol, 112 mg sodium, 123 mg potassium. Calories from protein: 14%; from carbohydrates: 68%; from fats: 18%.

CHALLAH

Challah, a traditional Jewish egg bread, is served in most Jewish homes for Sabbath meals and during festivals and holidays throughout the year. Its richness also makes it a good bread for toast and sandwiches.

2-CUP CAPACITY	INGREDIENTS	3-CUP CAPACITY
12 SERVINGS		**12 SERVINGS**
	YEAST	
2¼ teaspoons	Active dry yeast	SAME AS FOR 2-CUP CAPACITY
	DRY INGREDIENTS	
3 cups	Bread flour	
¾ teaspoon	Salt	
1 tablespoon	Granulated white sugar	
	LIQUID INGREDIENTS	
½ cup	Water	
2 large	Eggs	
1 large	Egg yolk	
3 tablespoons	Vegetable oil	
	EGG WASH	
1 large	Egg, beaten with 1 teaspoon water	
	TOPPING	
1 teaspoon	Poppy seeds	

MACHINE PROCEDURE: All ingredients must be at room temperature, unless otherwise noted. Add ingredients, except for egg wash and poppy seeds, in the order specified in your bread machine owner's manual. Set bread machine on dough/manual setting. At the end of the program, press clear/stop. To punch dough down, press start and let knead for 60 seconds. Press clear/stop again. Remove dough and let rest 5 minutes before hand-shaping.

If your bread machine does not have a dough/manual setting, follow normal bread making procedure but let dough knead only once. At the end of the kneading cycle, press clear/stop. Let dough rise for 60 minutes, checking after the first 30 minutes to make sure dough does not overrise and touch the lid. Press start and let machine run for

(continued on the next page)

60 seconds to punch the dough down. Press clear/stop. Remove dough and let rest 5 minutes before hand-shaping.

HAND-SHAPING TECHNIQUE: Lightly sprinkle work surface with flour. Divide dough into three equal pieces. Dampen hands and roll each piece into a 16-inch-long rope. Sprinkle dough with flour if too sticky. Lay ropes next to one another and pinch top ends together. Braid the ropes and pinch the remaining ends together. Place on a lightly greased 13- x 9- x 1-inch baking pan. Tuck ends under. Cover with a clean kitchen cloth and let rise until doubled in size, about 1 to 1½ hours.

Preheat oven to 375° F. Brush braid with egg wash and sprinkle with poppy seeds. Bake 30 minutes or until golden brown. Remove from oven and cool on wire rack.

Nutrition information per 1-inch slice:
126 calories, 3.53 g protein, 18.8 g carbohydrates, 0.75 g dietary fiber, 3.82 g fat, 39.9 mg cholesterol, 109 mg sodium, 42.1 mg potassium. Calories from protein: 11%; from carbohydrates: 61%; from fats: 28%.

Peppers and Egg, Broccoli and Cheese, and Salami and Cheese Pizza Roll-Ups and Calzones (pages 148, 149, and 145)

Fresh Herb Focaccia, Onion and Sage Focaccia, and Plum Tomato and Pecorino Romano Focaccia (pages 152, 153, and 154)

Basic, Onion, Poppy Seed, Sesame Seed, and Cinnamon Raisin Bagels (pages 176 and 178)

Chocolate, Cinnamon Sugar,
and Cheese Babkas
(pages 157, 156, and 158)

Zopf, Challah, and Easter Bread
(pages 120, 159, and 161)

Cinnamon Buns and Crumb Buns (pages 182 and 186)

Cheese, Fruit, and Nut and Raisin Danish (pages 188–190)

EASTER BREAD

Besides the lamb-shaped cakes with coconut frosting and jelly-bean eyes, every Easter I always remember the sweet yeast breads with the colored eggs in the center that we used to eat on Easter morning.

Begin a new tradition by baking and giving these colorful breads to family and friends.

2-CUP CAPACITY	INGREDIENTS	3-CUP CAPACITY
4 Servings		**4 Servings**
	YEAST	
2¼ teaspoons	Active dry yeast	SAME AS FOR 2-CUP CAPACITY
	DRY INGREDIENTS	
3 cups	Bread flour	
1 teaspoon	Grated lemon zest or crushed anise seed	
½ teaspoon	Salt	
3 tablespoons	Granulated white sugar	
4 tablespoons	Unsalted butter or margarine	
	LIQUID INGREDIENTS	
¾ cup	Milk	
2 large	Eggs	
	DECORATIONS	
4 large	Colored eggs, raw (eggs will cook in the oven while breads bake)	
2 teaspoons	Colored confettini sprinkles	
	EGG WASH	
1 large	Egg, beaten with 1 teaspoon water	

MACHINE PROCEDURE: All ingredients must be at room temperature, unless otherwise noted. Add ingredients in the order specified in your bread machine owner's manual. Set bread machine on dough/manual setting. At the end of the program, press clear/stop. To punch dough down, press start and let knead for 60 seconds. Press clear/stop again. Remove dough and let rest 5 minutes before hand-shaping.

If your bread machine does not have a dough/manual setting, follow normal bread

(continued on the next page)

Brioche, Petit Pain au Chocolat, and Petit Pain au Marmelade (pages 192, 194, and 195) making procedure, but let dough knead only once. At the end of the kneading cycle, press clear/stop. Let dough rise for 60 minutes, checking after the first 30 minutes to make sure dough does not overrise and touch lid. Press start and let machine run for 60 seconds to punch dough down. Press clear/stop. Remove dough and let rest 5 minutes before hand-shaping.

HAND-SHAPING TECHNIQUE: Lightly sprinkle work surface with flour. Divide dough into four equal pieces. Dampen hands and roll each piece into a 12-inch-long rope. Wrap each rope around a colored egg. Cross the ends, pinch together, and cut off any excess dough. Place on lightly greased 13- x 9- x 1-inch baking pan. Cover with a clean kitchen cloth and let rise until doubled in size, about 1 to 1½ hours.

Preheat oven to 375° F. Brush breads with egg wash, taking care not to get any on the colored eggs. Sprinkle with confettini sprinkles. Bake 25 to 30 minutes, or until a deep golden brown. Remove from oven and cool on wire rack.

Nutrition information per bread:
230 calories, 20.8 g protein, 83.5 g carbohydrates, 3.0 g dietary fiber, 21.4 g fat, 354 mg cholesterol, 647 mg sodium, 279 mg potassium. Calories from protein: 14%; from carbohydrates: 55%; from fats: 31%.

PROSCIUTTO CRACKED BLACK PEPPER BREAD

On Arthur Avenue in the Bronx, they make a fragrant yeast bread studded with chunks of prosciutto and cracked black pepper. Prosciutto is air-cured Italian ham made from the whole leg of the pig. It is lightly salted, pressed to remove most of the moisture, and then hung to cure for months. It has a delicate texture and flavor, which along with the coarsely ground black pepper in this recipe, makes for a remarkable bread.

Prosciutto has become readily available over the past few years and can be purchased in delicatessens, specialty food stores, and some supermarkets.

2-CUP CAPACITY 12 SERVINGS	INGREDIENTS	3-CUP CAPACITY 12 SERVINGS
	YEAST	SAME AS FOR 2-CUP CAPACITY
1½ teaspoons	Active dry yeast	
	DRY INGREDIENTS	
3 cups	Bread flour	
1 teaspoon	Salt	
1¼ teaspoons	Very coarsely ground black pepper	
	LIQUID INGREDIENTS	
1 cup	Water	
4 tablespoons	Melted vegetable shortening, cooled to room temperature	
	PROSCIUTTO	
½ cup	Coarsely chopped prosciutto (purchase a ¼-inch-thick slice and chop coarsely)	
	FOR BRUSHING	
	Vegetable oil	

MACHINE PROCEDURE: All ingredients must be at room temperature, unless otherwise noted. Add ingredients, except for prosciutto and vegetable oil, in the order specified in

(continued on the next page)

your bread machine owner's manual. Set bread machine on dough/manual setting. Add **prosciutto** 10 minutes after the kneading cycle begins. At the end of the first kneading, press clear/stop. Let dough rise for 60 minutes, checking after the first 30 minutes to make sure dough does not overrise and touch the lid. Press start to punch dough down. Let dough knead for 60 seconds. Press clear/stop again. Remove dough and let rest 5 minutes before hand-shaping.

If your bread machine does not have a dough/manual setting, follow normal bread making procedure, but let dough knead only once. Add **prosciutto** 10 minutes after the kneading cycle begins. At the end of the kneading cycle, press clear/stop. Let dough rise for 60 minutes, checking after first 30 minutes to make sure dough does not overrise and touch the lid. Press start and let machine run for 60 seconds to punch dough down. Press clear/stop again. Remove dough and let rest 5 minutes before hand-shaping.

HAND-SHAPING TECHNIQUE: Lightly sprinkle work surface with flour. Lightly sprinkle dough with flour and shape into a smooth ball. Poke a hole in the center of the dough and carefully stretch out into a large 8½-inch round, doughnut-like shape. The hole in the center should be approximately 4 inches in diameter. Place on a lightly greased 13- x 9- x 1-inch baking pan. Cover with a clean kitchen cloth and let rise until doubled in size, about 1 to 1½ hours.

Preheat oven to 400° F. Brush dough lightly with vegetable oil. Bake for approximately 30 minutes or until golden brown. Remove from oven and cool on a wire rack.

Nutrition information per 1-inch slice:
167 calories, 4.61 g protein, 24 g carbohydrates, 0.99 g dietary fiber, 5.57 g fat, 3.58 mg cholesterol, 248 mg sodium, 58.8 mg potassium. Calories from protein: 11%; from carbohydrates: 58%; from fats: 30%.

SWEDISH SAFFRON BREAD

For four years I worked as a coordinator for a foreign exchange organization. I was responsible for working with young European adults who were living with American families as au pairs. Besides being a rewarding experience, it also provided me with a great opportunity to acquire many new recipes, one of which was Swedish Saffron Bread.

Saffron bread is truly Swedish. Served in many different shapes and sizes, it is rich in color and flavor. It is best known as Lucia Bread and it is traditionally served by the eldest daughter to her family on the morning of December 13, St. Lucia Day.

This recipe was given me by Anna from Göteborg, a great baker according to her host family.

2-CUP CAPACITY	INGREDIENTS	3-CUP CAPACITY
16 SERVINGS		**16 SERVINGS**
	YEAST	
2¼ teaspoons	Fast-rise yeast	SAME AS FOR 2-CUP CAPACITY
	DRY INGREDIENTS	
3 cups	Unbleached all-purpose flour	
1 pinch	Salt	
⅓ cup	Granulated white sugar	
¼ teaspoon	Powdered saffron (see note)	
3 tablespoons	Unsalted butter or margarine	
	LIQUID INGREDIENTS	
¾ cup, plus 2 tablespoons	Milk	
1 large	Egg	
	EGG WASH	
1 large	Egg, beaten with 1 teaspoon water	
	DECORATION	
6	Blanched almonds	
6	Dark raisins	

MACHINE PROCEDURE: All ingredients must be at room temperature, unless otherwise noted. Add ingredients, except for egg wash and decorations, in the order specified in

(continued on the next page)

your bread machine owner's manual. Set bread machine on dough/manual setting. At the end of the program, press clear/stop. To punch dough down, press start and knead for 60 seconds. Press clear/stop again. Remove dough and let rest 5 minutes before hand-shaping.

If your bread machine does not have a dough/manual setting, follow normal bread making procedure, but let dough knead only once. At the end of the kneading cycle, press clear/stop. Let dough rise for 60 minutes, checking after the first 30 minutes to make sure dough does not overrise and touch the lid. Press start and let machine run for 60 seconds to punch dough down. Press clear/stop. Remove dough and let rest 5 minutes before hand-shaping.

HAND-SHAPING TECHNIQUE: Lightly sprinkle work surface with flour. Divide dough into two equal pieces. Lightly sprinkle with flour. Dampen hands and roll each piece into an 18-inch-long rope. Lay a rope on a lightly greased 13- x 9- x 1-inch baking pan. Lay second rope on top, forming a large X. Curl each end, toward center, into a coil. Cover with a clean kitchen cloth and let rise until doubled in size, about 1 to 1½ hours.

Preheat oven to 375° F. Brush bread with egg wash. Decorate the bread with the blanched almonds and raisins. Bake for approximately 25 to 30 minutes, or until golden brown. Remove from oven and cool on wire rack.

NOTE: Crush slightly less than ½ teaspoon saffron threads to make ¼ teaspoon powdered saffron.

Nutrition information per 1-inch slice:
154 calories, 4.3 g protein, 23.6 g carbohydrates, 1.03 g dietary fiber, 4.69 g fat, 34.4 mg cholesterol, 29.3 mg sodium, 83.4 mg potassium. Calories from protein: 11%; from carbohydrates: 61%; from fats: 27%.

PANETTONE

Rumor has it that many years ago in Italy, there was a baker's apprentice who was madly in love with the baker's daughter. Not happy with the situation, the baker told the apprentice that until he had something worthwhile to offer there would be no talk of marriage. The apprentice spent many a sleepless night until inspiration came to him in the form of a rich, sweet bread, chock full of dried fruits and flavored with rum. Needless to say, the rest is history. The story ends with the apprentice's name being revealed as Tony, which could easily explain the name of the bread as *pane di Tony*, which translates as "Tony's bread."

2-CUP CAPACITY	INGREDIENTS	3-CUP CAPACITY
16 Servings		**16 Servings**
	YEAST	
2¼ teaspoons	Fast-rise yeast	SAME AS FOR 2-CUP CAPACITY
	DRY INGREDIENTS	
3 cups	Unbleached all-purpose flour	
½ teaspoon	Salt	
¼ cup	Granulated white sugar	
1 teaspoon	Grated lemon zest	
6 tablespoons	Unsalted butter or margarine	
	LIQUID INGREDIENTS	
⅓ cup	Milk	
3 large	Eggs	
2 large	Egg yolks	
1½ teaspoons	Vanilla extract	
2 teaspoons	Dark rum	
	FRUITS	
⅓ cup	Coarsely chopped candied orange peel	
⅓ cup	Dark raisins	
⅓ cup	Golden raisins	
	BUTTER FOR BAKED BREAD	
1 teaspoon	Chilled unsalted butter	

(continued on the next page)

MACHINE PROCEDURE: All ingredients must be at room temperature, unless otherwise noted. Add ingredients, except fruits, in the order specified in your bread machine owner's manual. Set bread machine on dough/manual setting. Add **fruits** 10 minutes after pushing start. At the end of the first kneading cycle, press clear/stop. Let dough rise until doubled in size, about 1 to 1½ hours. Check every 30 minutes to make sure the dough does not overrise and touch lid. To punch dough down, press start and let knead for 60 seconds. Press clear/stop again. Remove dough and let rest 5 minutes before hand-shaping.

If your bread machine does not have a dough/manual setting, follow normal bread making procedure, but let dough knead only once. Add **fruits** 10 minutes after pushing start. At the end of the kneading cycle, press clear/stop. Let dough rise until doubled in size, about 1 to 1½ hours. Check every 30 minutes to make sure the dough does not overrise and touch the lid. Press start and let machine run for 60 seconds to punch dough down. Press clear/stop again. Remove dough and let rest 5 minutes before hand-shaping.

HAND-SHAPING TECHNIQUE: Lightly grease and flour a 9-inch cake pan or an 8-inch soufflé dish. Shape dough into a smooth ball and place in prepared pan. Tent a piece of lightly greased foil over pan. Let rise until dough reaches the top of the pan.

Preheat oven to 375° F. Remove foil and bake 35 to 40 minutes. If top begins to brown too quickly, loosely cover with a piece of foil. Remove from oven and pan. Cool on wire rack. Rub 1 teaspoon unsalted chilled butter over top and sides of baked, hot bread.

Nutrition information per ½-inch slice:
197 calories, 4.59 g protein, 28.9 g carbohydrates, 1.40 g dietary fiber, 7.06 g fat, 80.8 mg cholesterol, 83.9 mg sodium, 125 mg potassium. Calories from protein: 9%; from carbohydrates: 59%; from fats: 32%.

ZEPPOLE

A New York street fair just would not be complete without a brown paper bag of these hot, fried yeast doughnuts, heavily covered with confectioners' sugar.

This recipe was given to me by a friend who has had it written on a stained and yellowed file card for years. You can now enjoy zeppole more readily any time of the year, any place in the world. As with most fried confections, zeppole are best eaten within a short while after they are made—otherwise, they will become rubbery.

2-CUP CAPACITY ABOUT 24 ZEPPOLE	INGREDIENTS	3-CUP CAPACITY ABOUT 24 ZEPPOLE
	YEAST	
2¼ teaspoons	Fast-rise yeast	SAME AS FOR 2-CUP CAPACITY
	DRY INGREDIENTS	
2½ cups	Unbleached all-purpose flour	
½ teaspoon	Salt	
2 tablespoons	Granulated white sugar	
	LIQUID INGREDIENTS	
½ cup	Water	
2 large	Eggs	
	FOR FRYING	
4 cups	Vegetable oil	
	FOR DUSTING	
	Confectioners' sugar	

MACHINE PROCEDURE: All ingredients must be at room temperature, unless otherwise noted. Add ingredients, except for vegetable oil and confectioners' sugar, in the order specified in your bread machine owner's manual. Set bread machine on dough/manual setting. At the end of the program, press clear/stop. Dough will be sticky. To punch dough down, press start and knead for 60 seconds. Press clear/stop again. Let rest 5 minutes before hand-shaping.

If your bread machine does not have a dough/manual setting, follow normal bread making procedure, but let dough knead only once. At the end of the kneading cycle, press clear/stop. Dough will be sticky. Let dough rise for 60 minutes. Press start and let

(continued on the next page)

machine run for 60 seconds to punch dough down. Press clear/stop. Let rest 5 minutes before hand-shaping.

HAND-SHAPING TECHNIQUE: Heat 4 cups oil in a heavy-bottomed 2-quart saucepan. Using two teaspoons, drop teaspoonfuls of dough into hot oil. Dough will be sticky and elastic like taffy. Turn with a slotted spoon to brown evenly. Fry until a deep golden brown. Remove from oil with slotted spoon and drain on paper towels. You can fry 2 to 3 zeppole at a time. When cooled, sprinkle heavily with confectioners' sugar. Eat warm.

Nutrition information per Zeppola:
71 calories, 1.81 g protein, 12.1 g carbohydrates, 0.39 g dietary fiber, 1.60 g fat, 17.7 mg cholesterol, 50.1 mg sodium, 22.4 mg potassium. Calories from protein: 10%; from carbohydrates: 69%; from fats: 21%.

BEIGNETS

A trip to the French Market of New Orleans would not be complete without a stop at Café du Monde for a cup of café au lait and a serving of hot beignets covered with confectioners' sugar.

"Beignet" is French for "fritter," and in New Orleans the beignets are out of this world. As with most fried confections, beignets should be eaten within a short while after they are made—otherwise they will become rubbery.

2-CUP CAPACITY	INGREDIENTS	3-CUP CAPACITY
ABOUT 24 BEIGNETS		ABOUT 24 BEIGNETS
	YEAST	
2¼ teaspoons	Fast-rise yeast	SAME AS FOR 2-CUP CAPACITY
	DRY INGREDIENTS	
3 cups	Unbleached all-purpose flour	
1 teaspoon	Salt	
¼ cup	Granulated white sugar	
	LIQUID INGREDIENTS	
¾ cup, plus 2 tablespoons	Milk	
1 large	Egg	
2 tablespoons	Melted butter	
	FOR FRYING	
	Vegetable oil	
	FOR DUSTING	
	Confectioners' sugar	

MACHINE PROCEDURE: All ingredients must be at room temperature, unless otherwise noted. Add ingredients, except for vegetable oil and confectioners' sugar, in the order specified in your bread machine owner's manual. Set bread machine on dough/manual setting. At the end of the first kneading cycle, press clear/stop. Let dough rise until doubled in size, about 1 to 1½ hours. Check every 30 minutes to make sure the dough does not overrise and touch the lid. To punch dough down, press start and let knead for 60 seconds. Press clear/stop again. Remove dough and let rest 5 minutes before hand-shaping.

(continued on the next page)

If your bread machine does not have a dough/manual setting, follow normal bread making procedure, but let dough knead only once. At the end of the kneading cycle, press clear/stop. Let dough rise until doubled in size, about 1 to 1½ hours. Check every 30 minutes to make sure the dough does not overrise and touch the lid. Press start and let machine run for 60 seconds to punch dough down. Press clear/stop again. Remove dough and let rest 5 minutes before hand-shaping.

HAND-SHAPING TECHNIQUE: On lightly floured work surface roll dough into a ¼-inch-thick rectangle. Square off edges and cut dough into 2-inch squares. Heat 1 inch of oil in a heavy-bottomed skillet over medium heat. Fry beignets four at a time, turning with a slotted spoon, until puffed up and golden brown. Remove from pan with slotted spoon and drain on paper towels. While still warm, sprinkle with confectioners' sugar.

Nutrition information per Beignet:
100 calories, 2.24 g protein, 16.5 g carbohydrates, 0.50 g dietary fiber, 2.74 g fat, 12.6 mg cholesterol, 5.42 mg sodium, 37 mg potassium. Calories from protein: 9%; from carbohydrates: 66%; from fats: 25%.

DUTCH OLIEBOLLEN

To welcome in the New Year, Dutch families prepare and serve oliebollen, a delicious apple-and-raisin fritter-like doughnut. Rolled in granulated sugar, they are perfect to eat at breakfast all year round. As with most fried confections, oliebollen should be eaten within a short while after being made—otherwise they will become rubbery.

2-CUP CAPACITY	INGREDIENTS	3-CUP CAPACITY
ABOUT 24 OLIEBOLLEN		ABOUT 24 OLIEBOLLEN
	YEAST	
2¼ teaspoons	Fast-rise yeast	SAME AS FOR 2-CUP CAPACITY
	DRY INGREDIENTS	
2 cups	Unbleached all-purpose flour	
1 teaspoon	Salt	
1 tablespoon	Granulated white sugar	
	LIQUID INGREDIENTS	
¾ cup	Milk	
1 large	Egg	
	FRUIT	
½ cup	Dried black currants or raisins	
1 large	Tart apple, peeled, cored, and coarsely chopped	
	FOR FRYING	
	Vegetable oil	
	FOR DUSTING	
	Granulated white sugar	

MACHINE PROCEDURE: All ingredients must be at room temperature, unless otherwise noted. Add ingredients, except fruit, in the order specified in your bread machine owner's manual. Set bread machine on dough/manual setting. Add **fruits** 10 minutes after pressing start. At the end of the first kneading cycle, press clear/stop. Dough will be sticky. Let rise until doubled in size, about 1 to 1½ hours. Check every 30 minutes to make sure dough does not overrise and touch lid. To punch dough down, press start and let knead for 60 seconds. Press clear/stop again. Let rest 5 minutes before hand-shaping.

(continued on the next page)

If your bread machine does not have a dough/manual setting, follow normal bread making procedure, but let dough knead only once. Add **fruits** 10 minutes after pressing start. At the end of the kneading cycle, press clear/stop. Dough will be sticky. Let dough rise until doubled in size, about 1 to 1½ hours. Check every 30 minutes to make sure dough does not overrise and touch the lid. Press start and let machine run for 60 seconds to punch dough down. Press clear/stop again. Let rest 5 minutes before hand-shaping.

HAND-SHAPING TECHNIQUE: Heat 4 cups of oil in a heavy-bottomed 2-quart saucepan over medium heat. Using two teaspoons, drop teaspoonfuls of dough into hot oil. Dough will be very sticky and elastic like taffy. Turn with a slotted spoon to brown evenly. Remove from oil with slotted spoon and drain on paper towels. You can fry 2 to 3 oliebollen at a time. Roll them in granulated white sugar while they're still warm.

Nutrition information per Oliebollen:
77.9 calories, 1.99 g protein, 16.6 g carbohydrates, 0.89 g dietary fiber, 1.60 g fat, 17.7 mg cholesterol, 95 mg sodium, 88.1 mg potassium. Calories from protein: 10%; from carbohydrates: 84%; from fats: 6%.

BAGELS, BUNS, AND DANISH

It is unfortunate that breakfast, probably the most important meal of the day, is the least addressed by most people. More often than not, we grab a quick cup of coffee and some toast or perhaps a bowl of cereal with some fruit. This routine can become monotonous very quickly and some people even skip breakfast altogether. With a little planning, the recipes in this chapter, and the help of your automatic bread machine, breakfast does not have to be dull ever again.

Imagine enjoying homemade bagels, high in complex carbohydrates, with 0 grams of cholesterol and no added fat. Or better yet, wheat bagels that have the added value of 4.67 grams of dietary fiber. And for those special breakfasts or brunches, when no one is counting calories, mouthwatering, buttery, homemade Danish, cinnamon buns, or crumb buns.

Breakfast breads are fun, delicious, and easy to make. Since most of these recipes can be prepared the night before, you do not have to rush in the morning or take on a complicated task so early in the day. Only the Danish dough, which must rise in the refrigerator overnight, has to be finished up the next day.

BAGELS

Bagels do not need an introduction. This chewy, doughnut-shaped bread of Jewish origin is now known throughout the country.

In the mid-1980s, those unfortunate enough never to have eaten a bagel were finally able to do so through the introduction of frozen supermarket bagels. But there is no substitute for the real thing. Frozen bagels just do not have the chew and texture of hand-shaped, water-bath bagels. Boiling the bagels in water before they are baked reduces the starch and gives them their sheen and chewy texture. If for whatever reason you are hooked on softer-textured bagels, you can forgo the water-bath process and follow the instructions given for Glazed Bagels (page 180).

BASIC BAGELS

2-CUP CAPACITY 10 BAGELS	INGREDIENTS	3-CUP CAPACITY 10 BAGELS
	YEAST	
1¾ teaspoons	Active dry yeast	SAME AS FOR 2-CUP CAPACITY
	DRY INGREDIENTS	
3 cups	Bread flour	
1 teaspoon	Salt	
2 teaspoons	Dark brown sugar	
	LIQUID INGREDIENTS	
1 cup, plus 1 tablespoon	Water	

FOR SPRINKLING WORK SURFACE AND PAN
Finely ground cornmeal

FOR BOILING BAGELS
1 tablespoon   Dark brown sugar

SUGGESTED TOPPINGS (OPTIONAL)
Poppy seeds, sesame seeds,
finely minced garlic, reconstituted
dehydrated onions, or a mixture
of any of these

MACHINE PROCEDURE: All ingredients must be at room temperature, unless otherwise noted. Add ingredients, except topping, in the order specified in your bread machine owner's manual. Set bread machine on dough/manual setting. At the end of the first kneading, press clear/stop. Let dough rise for 60 minutes. Check after 30 minutes to be sure dough does not overrise and touch lid. Press start and let machine run for 60 seconds to punch dough down. Press clear/stop again. Remove dough and let rest 5 minutes before hand-shaping.

If your bread machine does not have a dough/manual setting, follow normal bread making procedure, but let dough knead only once. At the end of the kneading cycle, press clear/stop. Let dough rise for 60 minutes. Check after 30 minutes to be sure dough does not overrise and touch the lid. Press start and let machine run for 60 seconds to punch dough down. Press clear/stop. Remove dough and let rest 5 minutes before hand-shaping.

HAND-SHAPING TECHNIQUE: Lightly cover work surface with some of the cornmeal. Cut dough into ten equal pieces. Roll dough pieces into 10-inch-long ropes. Form each rope into a circle, overlapping the ends slightly. Fold right end over left end. Tuck under and pinch gently to hold together. Place shaped bagels on baking pans sprinkled with cornmeal. Cover with a clean kitchen cloth and let rest 30 minutes.

Preheat oven to 425° F. Bring 3 quarts of water to boil in large pot. Add 1 tablespoon of dark brown sugar. Using a large slotted spoon, drop bagels, three at a time, into the boiling water. Boil 3 minutes, turning periodically. Gently remove with slotted spoon and let dry on wire rack. When you have finished boiling all the bagels, place on baking pan sprinkled with cornmeal. Sprinkle with toppings if desired. Bake 15 minutes. Turn over and bake 10 more minutes, or until golden brown. Remove from oven and cool on wire rack.

Nutrition information per bagel (excluding toppings):
141 calories, 4.05 g protein, 29.5 g carbohydrates, 1.17 g dietary fiber, 0.38 g fat, 0 mg cholesterol, 429 mg sodium, 53.5 mg potassium. Calories from protein: 12%; from carbohydrates: 86%; from fats: 2%.

CINNAMON RAISIN BAGELS

For those of you who prefer the sweeter things in life, I recommend cinnamon raisin bagels.

Add ½ teaspoon ground cinnamon and ⅓ cup dark raisins to the Basic Bagel recipe, 5 minutes before the end of the kneading cycle.

Nutrition information per bagel (excluding toppings):
156 calories, 4.21 g protein, 33.4 g carbohydrates, 1.48 g dietary fiber, 0.402 g fat, 0 mg cholesterol, 429 mg sodium, 90 mg potassium. Calories from protein: 11%; from carbohydrates: 87%; from fats: 2%.

WHOLE-WHEAT BAGELS

Whole-wheat flour and honey give these bagels additional chew with the hearty flavor of whole grain.

2-CUP CAPACITY 10 BAGELS	INGREDIENTS	3-CUP CAPACITY 10 BAGELS
	YEAST	
1¾ teaspoons	Active dry yeast	SAME AS FOR 2-CUP CAPACITY
	DRY INGREDIENTS	
2 cups	Bread flour	
1 cup	Whole-wheat flour	
1 teaspoon	Salt	
	LIQUID INGREDIENTS	
1 cup, plus 1 tablespoon	Water	
2 tablespoons	Honey	

SUGGESTED TOPPINGS
Poppy seeds, sesame seeds, finely minced garlic, reconstituted dehydrated onions, or a mixture of any of these.

Follow the same machine procedure and hand-shaping technique as for Basic Bagels (page 176).

Nutrition information per bagel (excluding toppings):
146 calories, 4.41 g protein, 31.3 g carbohydrates, 2.34 g dietary fiber, 0.477 g fat, 0 mg cholesterol, 429 mg sodium, 87.7 mg potassium. Calories from protein: 12%; from carbohydrates: 85%; from fats: 3%.

GLAZED BAGELS

Glazed bagels are brushed with an egg wash rather than boiled in water before baking. The result is different, although equally as good.

INGREDIENTS

1 recipe Basic Bagels, Whole-Wheat Bagels, or Egg Bagels prepared up to point where bagels have risen on a baking pan sprinkled with finely ground cornmeal (see pages 176, 179, or 181 respectively)

EGG WASH GLAZE

1 large   Egg, beaten with
2 teaspoons water

SUGGESTED TOPPINGS

Poppy seeds, sesame seeds,
finely minced garlic, reconstituted
dehydrated onions, or a mixture
of any of these

Preheat oven to 375° F. Gently brush bagels with egg wash. Let dry 5 minutes. Brush again. Sprinkle with toppings if desired. Wait 10 minutes. Bake 20 minutes, or until a deep golden brown. Remove from oven and cool on wire rack.

Nutrition information per Bagel (excluding toppings):
141 calories, 4.05 g protein, 29.5 g carbohydrates, 1.17 g dietary fiber, 0.38 g fat, 0 mg cholesterol, 429 mg sodium, 53.5 mg potassium. Calories from protein: 12%; from carbohydrates: 86%; from fats: 2%.

EGG BAGELS

Although eggs are not a traditional addition, they make a lighter-textured bagel with a cheerful bright yellow color.

2-CUP CAPACITY	INGREDIENTS	3-CUP CAPACITY
10 BAGELS		**10 BAGELS**

YEAST

1¾ teaspoons	Active dry yeast	SAME AS FOR 2-CUP CAPACITY

DRY INGREDIENTS

3 cups	Bread flour
1 teaspoon	Salt
2 teaspoons	Dark brown sugar

LIQUID INGREDIENTS

¾ cup, plus 1 tablespoon	Water
1 large	Egg

SUGGESTED TOPPINGS

Poppy seeds, sesame seeds, finely minced garlic, reconstituted dehydrated onions, or a mixture of any of these

Follow the same machine procedure and hand-shaping technique as for Basic Bagels (see page 176).

Nutrition information per bagel (excluding toppings):
156 calories, 4.67 g protein, 31.3 g carbohydrates, 1.17 g dietary fiber, 0.88 g fat, 21.3 mg cholesterol, 435 mg sodium, 65.8 mg potassium. Calories from protein: 12%; from carbohydrates: 83%; from fats: 5%.

CINNAMON BUNS

Cinnamon buns are as American as apple pie. Every region of the country has its own favorite version. My favorite is made with mashed potatoes, which make the buns extra soft. Just keep in mind that cinnamon buns are best eaten the same day that they are made. (Allow at least one hour before making these buns to prepare the mashed potatoes.)

2-CUP CAPACITY 12 Servings	INGREDIENTS	3-CUP CAPACITY 12 Servings
	YEAST	
2¼ teaspoons	Fast-rise yeast	SAME AS FOR 2-CUP CAPACITY
	DRY INGREDIENTS	
1½ cups	Bread flour	
1½ cups	Unbleached all-purpose flour	
¼ cup	Granulated white sugar	
1 teaspoon	Salt	
1½ tablespoons	Nonfat dry milk	
2 tablespoons	Unsalted butter or margarine	
	LIQUID INGREDIENTS	
¾ cup, plus 2 tablespoons	Water	
¼ cup	Plain mashed potatoes (see note)	
1 large	Egg	
	BROWN SUGAR–CINNAMON FILLING	
⅓ cup	Dark brown sugar	
2 teaspoons	Ground cinnamon	
2 tablespoons	Unsalted butter, softened	

Mix brown sugar and cinnamon together. Reserve butter for spreading on risen dough.

	VANILLA FROSTING	
¼ cup	Unsalted butter, softened	
1 tablespoon	Unbleached all-purpose flour	
½ cup	Confectioners' sugar	
½ teaspoon	Vanilla extract	

Blend all ingredients together until smooth.

MACHINE PROCEDURE: All ingredients must be at room temperature, unless otherwise noted. Add ingredients except the filling and frosting in the order specified in your bread machine owner's manual. Set bread machine on dough/manual setting. At the end of the program, press clear/stop. To punch dough down, press start and let knead for 60 seconds. Press clear/stop again. Remove dough and let rest 5 minutes before hand-shaping.

If your bread machine does not have a dough/manual setting, follow normal bread making procedure, but let dough knead only once. At the end of the kneading cycle, press clear/stop. Let dough rise for 60 minutes, checking after the first 30 minutes to make sure dough does not overrise and touch the lid. Press start and let machine run for 60 seconds to punch dough down. Press clear/stop. Remove dough and let rest 5 minutes before hand-shaping.

HAND-SHAPING TECHNIQUE: Prepare filling and frosting and set aside. Generously sprinkle work surface with flour. Roll out dough into a 16- x 12-inch rectangle. Spread dough evenly with softened butter. Sprinkle with brown sugar–cinnamon filling. Roll up dough in jelly-roll fashion to form a 16-inch-long cylinder. With a sharp serrated knife, cut the cylinder into twelve equal slices. Place slices, cut side up, on two lightly greased 13- x 9- x 1-inch baking pans. Space 2 inches apart. Cover with a clean kitchen cloth and let rise 1 hour.

Preheat oven to 325° F. Bake buns for 10 minutes. Increase oven temperature to 350° F. Bake 5 minutes longer, or until lightly golden in color. Remove from oven. With a spatula remove the buns one at a time. Flip over on to waxed paper–covered wire racks. Cool completely. When cooled, spread with frosting.

NOTE: To make mashed potatoes, peel and quarter one medium (4-ounce) red potato. Boil until tender in unsalted water. Drain and mash potato with a fork until smooth. Cool to room temperature before using.

Nutrition information per bun:
252 calories, 4.35 g protein, 39.9 g carbohydrates, 1.16 g dietary fiber, 8.45 g fat, 38.6 mg cholesterol, 204 mg sodium, 96.3 mg potassium. Calories from protein: 7%; from carbohydrates: 63%; from fats: 30%.

HOT CROSS BUNS

"One-a-penny, two-a-penny, hot cross buns . . ." I guess we all heard this jingle at one time or another as children. These sweet harbingers of spring, with their sugar frosting crosses on the top, begin to appear in bakeries every year about a week before Lent.

Simple-to-make hot cross buns are a surefire way to ease into spring.

2-CUP CAPACITY **12 HOT CROSS BUNS**	INGREDIENTS	3-CUP CAPACITY **12 HOT CROSS BUNS**
	YEAST	
2¼ teaspoons	Active dry yeast	SAME AS FOR 2-CUP CAPACITY
	DRY INGREDIENTS	
3 cups	Bread flour	
½ teaspoon	Salt	
¼ cup	Granulated white sugar	
¼ teaspoon	Ground nutmeg	
¼ teaspoon	Ground cloves	
2 tablespoons	Unsalted butter or margarine	
	LIQUID INGREDIENTS	
¾ cup, less 1 tablespoon	Milk	
2 large	Eggs	
	RAISINS	
⅓ cup	Dark raisins	
	EGG WASH	
1 large	Egg white, beaten with 1 teaspoon water	
	FROSTING	
1 cup	Confectioners' sugar	
½ teaspoon	Vanilla extract	
3 tablespoons	Milk	

To make frosting, blend ingredients until smooth enough to use for piping.

MACHINE PROCEDURE: All ingredients must be at room temperature, unless otherwise noted. Add ingredients, except for raisins, egg wash, and frosting, in the order specified in your bread machine owner's manual. Set bread machine on dough/manual setting. Add **raisins** at the appropriate moment for your model bread machine. At the end of the program, press clear/stop. To punch dough down, press start and let knead for 60 seconds. Press clear/stop again. Remove dough and let rest 5 minutes before hand-shaping.

If your bread machine does not have a dough/manual setting, follow normal bread making procedure, but let dough knead only once. At the end of the kneading cycle, press clear/stop. Let dough rise for 60 minutes, checking after the first 30 minutes to make sure dough does not overrise and touch the lid. Press start and let machine run for 60 seconds to punch dough down. Press clear/stop. Remove dough and let rest 5 minutes before hand-shaping.

HAND-SHAPING TECHNIQUE: On lightly floured work surface, cut dough into three equal pieces. Lightly sprinkle dough with flour if too sticky to handle. Cut each piece into four pieces. Shape each piece into a smooth ball by stretching out and down a couple of times, always pinching together the bottom layer. Place buns on lightly greased 13- x 9- x 1-inch baking pan, four down and three across, with sides barely touching. Cover with a clean kitchen cloth and let rise until almost doubled in size, about 1 to 1½ hours.

Prepare frosting and set aside.

Preheat oven to 375° F. Gently brush buns with egg wash. Bake for 12 to 15 minutes or until lightly golden. Remove from oven and cool on wire racks. When cool, pipe a frosting cross on each bun.

Nutrition information per bun:
218 calories, 5.51 g protein, 40.5 g carbohydrates, 1.23 g dietary fiber, 3.75 g fat, 43.3 mg cholesterol, 115 mg sodium, 118 mg potassium. Calories from protein: 10%; from carbohydrates: 74%; from fats: 16%.

CRUMB BUNS

When I was growing up, Fisher's Bakery was the local meeting place on Sunday mornings. I'll never forget the buns they used to make with crumbs that would melt in your mouth and confectioners' sugar that would sprinkle all over your chin.

Fisher's Bakery is long gone, but the memory of their crumb buns still lingers.

2-CUP CAPACITY	INGREDIENTS	3-CUP CAPACITY
9 Servings		**9 Servings**
	YEAST	
2¼ teaspoons	Fast-rise yeast	SAME AS FOR 2-CUP CAPACITY
	DRY INGREDIENTS	
2½ cups	Bread flour	
¾ teaspoon	Salt	
¼ cup	Granulated white sugar	
2 tablespoons	Unsalted butter or margarine	
	LIQUID INGREDIENTS	
½ cup, plus 1 tablespoon	Milk	
½ teaspoon	Vanilla extract	
1 large	Egg	
	CRUMB TOPPING	
½ cup	Unbleached all-purpose flour	
¼ cup	Dark brown sugar	
1 tablespoon	Granulated white sugar	
2 pinches	Ground cinnamon	
¼ cup	Unsalted butter or margarine, softened	
	FOR DUSTING	
	Confectioners' sugar	

MACHINE PROCEDURE: All ingredients must be at room temperature, unless otherwise noted. Add ingredients, except the topping and confectioners' sugar, in the order specified in your bread machine owner's manual. Set bread machine on dough/manual setting. At the end of the program, press clear/stop. To punch dough down, press start and let knead for 60 seconds. Press clear/stop again. Remove dough and let rest 5 minutes before hand-shaping.

If your bread machine does not have a dough/manual setting, follow normal bread making procedure, but let dough knead only once. At the end of the kneading cycle, press clear/stop. Let dough rise for 60 minutes, checking after the first 30 minutes to make sure dough does not overrise and touch the lid. Press start and let machine run for 60 seconds to punch dough down. Press clear/stop. Remove dough and let rest 5 minutes before hand-shaping.

HAND-SHAPING TECHNIQUE: Prepare topping. In a medium-size mixing bowl, combine all the dry ingredients. Mix well. With two butter knives, cut in butter or margarine until pea-size crumbs form. Refrigerate until ready to use.

Place dough in a lightly buttered 9-inch-square baking pan. Gently press dough with fingertips to spread evenly. Cover with a clean kitchen cloth. Let rise until doubled in size.

Preheat oven to 350° F. Make light indentations with fingertips in the surface of the risen dough. Sprinkle crumb mixture evenly over dough. Bake for approximately 30 minutes, or until crumbs are lightly browned and firm. Remove from oven and cool on wire rack. When completely cooled, sprinkle with confectioners' sugar. Cut into nine equal squares.

Nutrition information per bun:
288 calories, 5.73 g protein, 45.4 g carbohydrates, 1.26 g dietary fiber, 9.15 g fat, 46.4 mg cholesterol, 197 mg sodium, 107 mg potassium. Calories from protein: 8%; from carbohydrates: 63%; from fats: 29%.

DANISH

Perfectly shaped glazed Danish pastries topped with luscious fillings can easily be made at home. Since your bread machine will be doing all the hard work making the somewhat sticky and heavy dough, you need only concern yourself with shaping the chilled dough into mini-masterpieces.

For the Danish to come out light and buttery, the dough must be chilled for at least 12 hours before shaping. The Danish pastries can then be topped with a wide variety of toppings. I have included a few personal favorites for you to sample.

BASIC DANISH DOUGH

2-CUP CAPACITY	INGREDIENTS	3-CUP CAPACITY
18 SERVINGS		**18 SERVINGS**
	DRY INGREDIENTS	
4 teaspoons	Active dry yeast	SAME AS
3½ cups	Unbleached all-purpose flour	FOR 2-CUP
2 teaspoons	Salt	CAPACITY
¼ cup	Granulated white sugar	
1½ cups	Cold unsalted butter, cut into 24 small pieces	
	LIQUID INGREDIENTS	
1 cup	Milk	
2 large	Eggs	
	EGG WASH	
1 large	Egg, beaten with 1 teaspoon water	
	ICING	
1½ cups	Confectioners' sugar	
3 tablespoons	Water	
½ teaspoon	Vanilla extract, dark rum, or brandy	

MACHINE PROCEDURE: Add dry ingredients in the above given order. Press start and knead until butter is cut into dry ingredients and dough appears coarse and crumbly. Gradually add liquid ingredients. Knead for 5 to 10 minutes or until ingredients appear well mixed. *Do not* overknead. Press stop. Dough will be soft and very sticky.

Place dough in large, well-buttered mixing bowl. Tightly cover with plastic wrap or foil and place in refrigerator for at least 12 hours.

HAND-SHAPING TECHNIQUE: Preheat oven to 400° F. On a lightly floured work surface cut dough into eighteen equal pieces. Roll each piece into a 16-inch-long rope. Loosely coil each rope, tucking end under coil. Place on baking pans covered with parchment paper. Space 2 inches apart. Cover with a clean kitchen cloth and let rise for 30 minutes.

Prepare filling of your choice and set aside. Combine icing ingredients and set aside. Form a 2-inch-wide well in the center of each Danish by gently pressing down with fingertips. Fill the well with desired filling. Brush Danish with egg wash. Bake approximately 12 to 14 minutes or until golden brown. Remove from baking sheet and cool on wire racks. Lightly glaze with icing while still warm.

CHEESE DANISH FILLING

8 ounces	Cream cheese
¼ cup	Granulated white sugar
¼ cup	Unbleached all-purpose flour
1 large	Egg yolk
2 teaspoons	Grated orange zest

Mix all ingredients until well combined. Refrigerate until ready to use.

Nutrition information per Cheese Danish:
353 calories, 5.62 g protein, 34.8 g carbohydrates, 0.89 g dietary fiber, 21.6 g fat, 104 mg cholesterol, 295 mg sodium, 91.5 mg potassium. Calories from protein: 6%; from carbohydrates: 39%; from fats: 55%.

FRUIT DANISH FILLING

1 tablespoon	Cornstarch
2 teaspoons	Lemon juice
1 16-ounce	Can of fruit in light syrup (sliced cling peaches, apricot halves, or crushed pineapple), drained; reserve 3 tablespoons syrup
¼ cup	Granulated white sugar

In a small heavy-bottomed saucepan, stir together cornstarch, lemon juice, and 3 tablespoons of fruit syrup. Mix well until smooth. Add remaining ingredients. Cook over low heat, stirring occasionally until thick. Cool to room temperature.

(continued on the next page)

NUT AND RAISIN DANISH FILLING

1 cup	Very finely chopped walnuts, almonds, hazelnuts, or any combination of these
¼ cup	Dark raisins
¼ cup	Granulated white sugar
1 teaspoon	Ground cinnamon
2 tablespoons	Unsalted butter, softened
2 large	Egg whites, lightly beaten

Mix all ingredients until well combined. Refrigerate until ready to use.

BRIOCHE, PETITS PAINS, AND DOUGHNUTS

Brioche is definitely not for calorie counters or the uninitiated. The grande dame of French yeast dough, brioche is extremely high in fat, which gives it its rich texture when baked. Nevertheless, a bread cookbook would be incomplete without at least one delectable basic brioche recipe. Despite being "nutritively incorrect," brioche should not be dismissed but instead should be respected and made at the appropriate moment when a special occasion arises.

Traditionally baked in small, fluted metal tins, brioche resemble small rolls with tiny knobs of dough attached to the top. Delicious when served with jam or preserves and a steaming cup of coffee, basic brioche dough has innumerable uses.

Making brioche by hand is time-consuming and requires a certain level of skill. While your bread machine will do most of the hard work, it will be necessary for you to assist along the way. Since brioche is a very soft, butter- and egg-enriched dough, you have to proceed slowly when adding the ingredients to the operating bread machine. This may require that you gently push the dough down periodically with a spatula so that the ingredients mix in well.

Once you taste your first brioche, you will agree that this is the finest of yeast breads.

BRIOCHE

Brioche is a classic French yeast dough made with eggs and butter. This wonderfully adaptable dough can be used to make rolls, loaves, and even doughnuts. It is also a perfect cover for other delectable ingredients such as bittersweet chocolate and home-made preserves.

Although this dough requires some assistance from you, the baker, it is well worth making, as I am sure you will agree.

2-CUP CAPACITY 10 SERVINGS	INGREDIENTS	3-CUP CAPACITY 10 SERVINGS
	YEAST	
2¼ teaspoons	Active dry yeast	SAME AS FOR 2-CUP CAPACITY
	DRY INGREDIENTS	
1½ cups	Bread flour	
1½ cups	Unbleached all-purpose flour	
1 teaspoon	Salt	
2 tablespoons	Granulated white sugar	
12 tablespoons	Unsalted butter, softened and cut into 12 pieces (added to dough in three separate batches of 4 tablespoons each, sprinkled lightly with flour)	
	LIQUID INGREDIENTS	
⅓ cup, plus 1 tablespoon	Milk	
3 large	Eggs	
	ADDITIONAL FLOUR	
3 tablespoons	Unbleached all-purpose flour	
	EGG WASH	
1 large	Egg, beaten with 1 teaspoon water	

MACHINE PROCEDURE: All ingredients must be at room temperature, unless otherwise noted. Add ingredients in the order specified in your bread machine owner's manual. Add only 4 tablespoons butter to start. Set bread machine on dough/manual setting. After butter is mixed in, add another 4 tablespoons; when mixed in, add remaining butter. Dough will be very sticky. Add additional 3 tablespoons of flour, 1 tablespoon at a time, to the side of the pan where most of the dough is kneading. If necessary, press down on dough with spatula to help mix in flour. Dough will come together in a soft ball. At the end of the program, press clear/stop. To punch dough down, press start and let knead for 60 seconds. Press clear/stop again. Remove dough and let rest 5 minutes before hand-shaping.

If your bread machine does not have a dough/manual setting, follow normal bread making procedure, but let dough knead only once. At the end of the kneading cycle, press clear/stop. Let dough rise for 60 minutes, checking after the first 30 minutes to make sure dough does not overrise and touch the lid. Press start and let machine run for 60 seconds to punch dough down. Press clear/stop again. Remove dough and let rest 5 minutes before hand-shaping.

HAND-SHAPING TECHNIQUE: Lightly flour work surface. Divide dough into twelve equal pieces. Divide two of the pieces into five smaller pieces each. Shape into small balls. Put aside. Lightly butter ten individual brioche molds or a cupcake pan. Shape remaining ten pieces of dough into smooth, tight balls by stretching out and down a couple of times, always pinching together the bottom edges. Place in molds or pan. Make an indentation with your thumb on top of each brioche. Wet indentation with some of the egg wash. Top with one of the small reserved balls of dough. Cover with a clean kitchen cloth and let rise until doubled in size, about 1 to 1½ hours.

Preheat oven to 375° F. Brush brioches with egg wash. Make certain egg wash does not drip down the sides or it may be difficult to remove the brioches from the molds or pan when done. Bake approximately 20 minutes or until a deep golden brown. Remove and cool on wire racks.

Nutrition information per Brioche:
258 calories, 5.63 g protein, 28.5 g carbohydrates, 1.08 g dietary fiber, 13.4 g fat, 85.4 mg cholesterol, 199 mg sodium, 77.7 mg potassium. Calories from protein: 9%; from carbohydrates: 44%; from fats: 47%.

PETIT PAIN AU CHOCOLAT

In another time, French schoolchildren would stop at the local baker on the way to school to drop off a piece of semisweet chocolate. The baker would wrap the chocolate in scraps of brioche dough. After school the children would pick up their afternoon snack, a delectable *petit pain au chocolat*.

8 SERVINGS

INGREDIENTS

1 recipe Brioche dough chilled for at least 4 hours or overnight (see page 192)

CHOCOLATE FILLING

8 ounces	Semisweet chocolate bar, preferably imported, broken into squares

EGG WASH

1 large	Egg, beaten with 1 teaspoon water

MACHINE PROCEDURE: Prepare Brioche dough (see page 192).

HAND-SHAPING TECHNIQUE: Lightly sprinkle work surface with flour. Cut dough into two equal pieces. Roll each piece of dough into a 16- x 4-inch rectangle. Square off the edges. Cut each piece into four squares. Place two squares of chocolate in the center of each piece of dough. Brush edges with egg wash and fold dough over to form a package. Pinch edges together. Place on lightly greased 13- x 9- x 1-inch baking pan, seam side down. Fold edges under. Press down gently to flatten slightly. Cover with a clean kitchen cloth and let rise 1 hour.

Preheat oven to 375° F. Brush petits pains with egg wash and bake for 20 minutes or until golden brown. Remove from oven and cool on wire rack.

Nutrition information per petit pain:
508 calories, 7.92 g protein, 58.0 g carbohydrates, 2.47 g dietary fiber, 29 g fat, 74.9 mg cholesterol, 288 mg sodium, 198 mg potassium. Calories from protein: 6%; from carbohydrates: 44%; from fats: 50%.

PAIN AU MARMELADE

Pain au marmelade is a rich dessert confection to be enjoyed with a cup of coffee or tea. Use the best fruit preserves you can find for a wonderful taste experience.

12 SERVINGS

INGREDIENTS

1 recipe Brioche dough, chilled for at least 4 hours or overnight (see page 192)

FRUIT FILLING

½ cup   Fruit preserves (good quality)

EGG WASH

1 large   Egg, beaten with
                  1 teaspoon water

MACHINE PROCEDURE: Prepare 1 recipe Brioche dough (see page 192).

HAND-SHAPING TECHNIQUE: Lightly sprinkle work surface with flour. Cut dough into two equal pieces. Roll each piece of dough into a 12- x 6-inch rectangle. Spread the fruit preserves on one of the rectangles, leaving a 1-inch border along the edges. Brush edges with egg wash. Cover with the other rectangle of dough and crimp edges to seal. Carefully place on lightly greased 13- x 9- x 1-inch baking pan. Cover with a clean kitchen cloth and let rise 1 hour.

Preheat oven to 375° F. Brush pain au marmelade with egg wash. Prick in a decorative pattern a few times with a fork. Bake for 20 to 25 minutes, or until golden brown. Remove from oven and cool on wire rack. When cool, cut into twelve slices.

Nutrition information per 1-inch slice:
279 calories, 4.58 g protein, 37.2 g carbohydrates, 1.17 g dietary fiber, 12.5 g fat, 49.9 mg cholesterol, 191 mg sodium, 78.0 mg potassium. Calories from protein: 7%; from carbohydrates: 53%; from fats: 40%.

BRIOCHE·DOUGHNUTS

I feel almost guilty including this recipe, since it is so rich and high in calories. But it is so good you should at least try it once without any remorse.

APPROXIMATELY 18 DOUGHNUTS

INGREDIENTS
1 recipe Brioche dough, chilled for at least 4 hours or overnight (see page 192)

FOR FRYING
Vegetable oil

FOR DUSTING
Confectioners' sugar

MACHINE PROCEDURE: Prepare 1 recipe Brioche dough (see page 192).

HAND-SHAPING TECHNIQUE: On lightly floured work surface, roll out dough into a ½-inch-thick rectangle. With a 2-inch diameter biscuit cutter or glass, cut out as many circles as possible. Heat 1 inch of oil in a heavy-bottomed, deep skillet over medium heat. Fry until golden brown, turning over to brown evenly. Remove with slotted spoon. Drain on paper towels. Cool on wire racks. Sprinkle on all sides with confectioners' sugar.

Nutrition information per doughnut:
182 calories, 2.65 g protein, 21.3 g carbohydrates, 0.70 g dietary fiber, 9.58 g fat, 21.4 mg cholesterol, 123 mg sodium, 40.8 mg potassium. Calories from protein: 6%; from carbohydrates: 47%; from fats: 47%.

THE INSIDER'S GUIDE TO
PERFECT BREAD AND DOUGH

For best results, read and refer to the Introduction, especially The Insider's Guide to Making Bread Automatically (page 13), Taking It to the Next Step (page 16), and Ingredients and Tools of the Trade (page 17).

PROBLEM:
Bread machine labors during kneading cycle.
OR Dough does not come together into a ball.

REASON:
Dough is too dry because:
1. Amount of ingredients exceeds manufacturer's recommendations. Check owner's manual for appropriate amount.
2. Recipe contains ingredients that will absorb water if used with programmable timer.
3. Recipe has puréed fruits or vegetables or whole grains that may require that additional water be added.
4. Water is hard.
5. Small or medium eggs were used.

SOLUTION:
1. Add additional water, 1 tablespoon at a time, until dough appears smooth and elastic.
2. Use programmable timer only when specified. See Solution 1 for remedy.
3. See Solution 1 for remedy.
4. Use an alternative source of water.
5. Only use large eggs.

PROBLEM:
Dough is very sticky.

REASON:
1. Flour has high moisture content.
2. Too much liquid was used.
3. Water is soft.
4. Extra-large or jumbo eggs were used.

SOLUTION:
1. If problem is ongoing, change brand of flour.
2. Add additional flour, 1 tablespoon at a time, until dough appears smooth and elastic.
3. Use an alternative source of water.
4. Only use large eggs.

PROBLEM:
Dough bread did not rise high enough.

REASON:
1. Ingredients were not at the appropriate temperature, as specified in the recipe.
2. Ingredients were not put in the bread pan in the order specified by the manufacturer in the owner's manual.
3. Yeast did not activate.
4. Low-gluten flour was used.
5. High altitude.
6. Hard water.
7. Ambient temperature was below 68° F.

SOLUTION:
1. Ingredients must be at room temperature unless otherwise specified.
2. Ingredients must be put in the bread pan in the order recommended by the manufacturer. Refer to the owner's manual.
3. Be sure yeast is fresh; check expiration date on back of yeast package or jar. If past expiration date, dough will not rise.
4. Only use **high-gluten** bread or unbleached all-purpose flour, unless otherwise specified.
5. If baking at an altitude 3000 feet above sea level, reduce the water by 1 tablespoon for every 1000 feet above 3000. Do not decrease by more than 4 tablespoons. If dough appears to be too dry, add back some of the water, a tablespoon at a time, until the dough appears smooth and elastic.
6. Use an alternative source of water.
7. Use bread machine in a location that is 68° F to 75° F.

PROBLEM:
Dough bread touches the top of bread machine lid.

REASON:
1. Weather very hot and/or humid.
2. Too much yeast was used.
3. Wrong kind of yeast was used.

SOLUTION:
1. Make dough or bread only when ambient temperature is between 68° to 80° F. Try reducing yeast by 25 to 33 percent.
2. Use only the amount of yeast specified in the recipe for the appropriate-size bread machine.
3. Use the appropriate kind of yeast specified in the recipe. Do not substitute fast-rise yeast for active dry.

PROBLEM:
Bread collapses when baked.

Dough rose unevenly because of:

1. Excess moisture.
2. Too much water.
3. High water temperature, causing dough to proof unevenly.

SOLUTION:

1. Since flour is extremely absorbent, it will absorb excess moisture from the air during periods of high humidity. Reduce water in recipes by 2 to 3 tablespoons.
2. Measure water carefully. Use only amount specified in recipe.
3. Make sure water temperature does not exceed 80° F.

PROBLEM:
Bread does not bake completely.

REASON:

1. Ingredients were not measured properly.
2. Ambient temperature was lower than 68° F.
3. Bread machine lid was not closed.

SOLUTION:

1. Measure ingredients with U.S. standard measuring cups and spoons. Spoon flour into measuring cups. Level off with a blunt-ended knife.
2. Room too cold and dough did not develop properly. Use in warmer location.
3. Make bread only with lid down at all times.

PROBLEM:
Bread burns.

REASON:

1. Baking temperature too high.
2. Recipe was modified.

SOLUTION:

1. If possible, set bread machine on lighter setting, or if baking in a conventional oven, lower the temperature.
2. Reduce amount of sweetener and fat by 20 percent.

PROBLEM:
Dough does not stretch during hand-shaping.

REASON:

1. Dough is too dry.
2. Gluten needs to rest.

SOLUTION:

1. Always make sure that dough is smooth and elastic while kneading. If not, add additional water, 1 tablespoon at a time, until dough appears smooth and elastic.
2. Never try to hand-shape or roll dough out right after kneading. Dough needs to rest to relax the gluten so that it will stretch sufficiently.

PROBLEM:

Dough does not rise.

REASON:

1. Yeast is more than a year old or is inactive because of poor storage.
2. You forgot to add the yeast.
3. Dough is rich with sugar, eggs, and fats.

SOLUTION:

1. Always check the expiration date on the back of the yeast package. Opened packages of yeast should be stored in airtight containers in either the refrigerator or the freezer.
2. Dough cannot rise without a leavening agent.
3. Doughs rich with sugar, eggs, and fats will rise much slower. Cover and let rise in undisturbed, draft-free, warm location.

PROBLEM:

Ingredients like raisins, dried fruits, and nuts become chopped up and do not come out whole after the bread has baked.

REASON:

You did not add them at the appropriate moment for your model bread machine.

SOLUTION:

If your bread machine has a special cycle for adding ingredients like dried fruits and nuts, use it. If not, add 10 minutes before the end of the final kneading cycle.

PROBLEM:

Ingredients like raisins, dried fruits, and nuts do not incorporate well into the dough and stick to the sides or bottom of the baked bread or dough.

REASON:

1. Ingredients were added too late and bread machine did not have enough time to fold them into dough.
2. Dough was too dry and could not stretch enough to incorporate additional ingredients.

SOLUTION:

1. Try adding dried fruits and nuts a minute or two sooner.
2. Try adding additional water to the dough the next time you make this recipe. Add the water a tablespoon at a time, until the dough is smooth and elastic.

SOURCE DIRECTORY

ALTHOUGH ALMOST ALL OF THE INGREDIENTS you will ever need to make excellent loaves of quality breads and confections are available at your local supermarket, the following three mail order companies are useful sources of hard-to-find grains, flours, spices, and other baking-related ingredients and accessories.

King Arthur Flour Baker's Catalogue
Sands, Taylor & Wood Company
Box 1010
Norwich, Vermont 05055
(800)827–6836

This has to be the ultimate baker's ingredients and accessories catalogue. Established in 1790, King Arthur Flour Baker's Catalogue offers a near endless variety of flours, herbs, spices, and accessories. Even if you do not buy anything, it's great just knowing that they are out there.

The Great Valley Mills
RD 3, County Line Road
Box 1111
Barto, PA 19504
(800)688–6455

Established in 1710 as a grist mill, the Great Valley Mills offers a catalogue with a wide variety of high-quality, family-grown-and-produced foods and grains from Lancaster County, Pennsylvania. An excellent source of quality stone-ground flours.

Williams-Sonoma
P.O. Box 7456
San Francisco, CA 94120–7456
(800)541–2233

This catalogue calls itself *A Catalog for Cooks*, which is an understatement. An excellent source for all types of quality housewares and food products. Good selection of sun-dried tomatoes, flavored oils, and dried fruits.

INDEX